Poems of Devotion

"The phrase 'contemporary devotional poetry' is more likely to conjure images of treacly holiday greeting cards than literature of the highest order. But this anthology, on the contrary, bears witness to the perennial human desire to adore—and to question, Job-like—the Almighty. This is a generous and inclusive selection, containing not only modern masters but also emerging voices. Above all, it is a reminder that the best writing is, in the end, an offering to the Mystery."

—Gregory Wolfe, editor of *Image*

Poems of Devotion

An Anthology of Recent Poets

Edited with an Introduction
by Luke Hankins

WIPF & STOCK · Eugene, Oregon

POEMS OF DEVOTION
An Anthology of Recent Poets

Wipf & Stock
An Imprint of Wipf and Stock Publishers
199 W. 8th Ave., Suite 3
Eugene, OR 97401

www.wipfandstock.com

ISBN 13: 978-1-61097-712-8

Manufactured in the U.S.A.

Cover art: "Thirsting" (24" x 48" encaustic on panel) by G. Carol Bomer, used by permission of the artist. www.carolbomer.com

All scripture quotations, unless otherwise indicated, are taken from the Holy Bible, New International Version®, NIV®. Copyright ©1973, 1978, 1984 by Biblica, Inc.™ Used by permission of Zondervan. All rights reserved worldwide.

The introductory essay, "The Poem as Devotional Practice: The Lasting Model of the 17th-century Religious Poets," appeared in an earlier version in *Contemporary Poetry Review*. The appended interview originally appeared on the *American Literary Review* blog.

Contents

Contents

Contents

Contents

Personal Thanks

My gratitude to Esme Franklin, who helped enormously with the preparation of this anthology.

A special thanks to Ron Rios of Black Mountain, NC, for his financial support of this project.

Thank you to all those who contributed money through Kickstarter to help with the permissions fees for this project.

I am also grateful to Stephen Haven, Hannah Faith Notess, Don Share, Sofia Starnes, Daniel Westover, John Wood, and any others I've forgotten to mention who offered suggestions and other assistance.

Introduction

The Poem as Devotional Practice

The Lasting Model of the 17th-century Poets

by Luke Hankins

I. A Lasting Model?

CERTAIN RELIGIOUS POETS OF 17th-century England, often called the "Metaphysical" poets, have gained as firm a place in the Western canon as any group of poets enjoys today. Tangibly speaking, that means that they (at least the major four or five) are ubiquitously anthologized, their work remains in print and readily available, there exists a large body of critical work on their poetry and lives, and they are regularly "taught" in post-secondary classrooms, as well as in at least some secondary class-rooms. It is clear that they have some measure of significance for scholars, but what influence, if any, do they exert on literature in America today?[1]

II. Defining Devotional Poetry

In reference to 17th-century poets, the term "Metaphysical" has come to indicate cer-tain stylistic tendencies, such as elaborately extended metaphor or conceit, fondness for paradox, and linguistic inventiveness and ingenuity (often loosely termed "wit"). It is strange, considering the etymology of this word and its uses in other contexts, that it should have come to designate stylistic rather than philosophical or spiritual elements. The word was Latinized from Greek in the Middle Ages, and the Latin roots of the word, *meta* and *physic*, might be rendered "over/above" and "nature/the natural," thus indicating the supernatural, the spiritual, or at least the philosophical.[2] In fact, the

---

1. My focus in this essay and in this volume will be on recent literature written in the United States, but it will also include some work from other countries that is either widely read in the U.S. or that I think should be more widely read here.

2. All etymologies discussed in this essay refer to information found in *The Oxford English Dictionary*.

Greek phrase from which the Latin was derived was used as early as the 4th century B.C. as a title for one of Aristotle's treatises, on the subject of ontological philosophy.[3]

However, since Samuel Johnson's largely pejorative remarks about the aims of the "metaphysical" poets, the word has become associated with those stylistic characteristics of the verse that he found offensive or inadequate.[4] We now use the terms "religious" or "devotional" when we want to indicate these poets' spiritual practice and subject matter—though, as I hope to demonstrate, these two terms are not interchangeable, devotional poetry being a specific mode within the larger category of religious poetry.

Anthony Low has done important work in studying 17th-century devotional practice and its relation to the poetry of the time. In his book, *Love's Architecture: Devotional Modes in Seventeenth-century English Poetry*, he indicates four primary types of devotional practice—vocal, meditative, affective, and contemplative—and demonstrates the ways in which these spiritual exercises influenced the verse of the poets of that age. It often seems implicit in Low's commentary on the poems of the era that the poems are not only informed by or imitative of devotional practice, but are themselves part of that devotional practice, but he does not state this explicitly. Let us state it explicitly, and proceed to support the notion: The composition of a poem may itself be a devotional practice.

We are not likely to be able to know for certain to what extent any given poem was composed as a devotional practice, as opposed to being a re-creation of prior devotional practice or explanation of the outcomes thereof; however, the idea that a poem *can* be a devotional practice is significant and bears being stated and defended. In his essay, "Metaphysical Poets and Devotional Poets," Low says that "Metaphysical poetry is essentially private poetry, that is, poetry that examines and focuses on the inner movements of thought and feeling,"[5] but he comes short of saying that a poem itself can be *a way of thinking*. "In its combination of reason, imagination, and feelings," he goes on to say, "meditation is a close cousin of poetry,"[6] and yet he does not acknowledge poetry as *a means of meditating*. The implication of statements of this kind (wittingly or no on Low's part) is that poetry is a recorder of other, prior processes. Literary critics tend to speak this way when they are not thinking like writers. If they were to stop for a moment to consider their own processes in composing their essays or books, they might revise the way they speak of poems, for

3. "Metaphysical," *Oxford English Dictionary*.

4. John Dryden had made remarks that were even more hostile in the previous century, but he did not designate the poets as "metaphysical," though he did speak of Donne "affect[ing] the metaphysics" (*The Metaphysical Poets*, 121).

5. Low, "Metaphysical Poets and Devotional Poets," 224.

6. Ibid., 228.

even an essay is not simply the writing down of fully-formed thoughts, but is a way of organizing and exploring and furthering thought, and is revised in light of the discoveries made in the process of writing.

In his essay, "The Shocking Image," A. D. Nutall says, referring to 17th-century handbooks offering instruction in devotional practice, "The handbooks taught that a man [sic] should train his imagination as an athlete trains his body. It is natural that such a system should produce certain champions, gymnasts of the imagination, whose powers should spill over into their poetry."[7] But Nutall misses the mark when he says that the powers of imagination merely "spill over" into poetry. It makes far more sense to understand the composition of poetry as itself an act of imagination—in other words, not only the *result* of imaginative training, but part of the training itself. Low and Nutall have overlooked the possibility that the composition of a poem can itself be an act of devotion, rather than merely chronicling or imitating or being otherwise influenced by devotional practice. In order to understand this, it is vital to realize that poems are not necessarily begun as foregone conclusions, and, in fact, it would be unlikely for such a poem to prove a lasting work of literature.

Robert Frost famously said that a poem "is but a trick poem and no poem at all if the best of it was thought of first and saved for the last," and that "like a piece of ice on a hot stove the poem must ride on its own melting. [. . .] It can never lose its sense of a meaning that once unfolded by surprise as it went."[8] Great poems are—if not invariably, at least most often—an unfolding, not only for the reader, but for the poet in the process of composing.

George Herbert, more consistently than any other 17th-century poet, gives the reader the sense that he is struggling through the poem itself, that the poem is a tool by which he does his thinking. Take this middle section from "The Search," for instance:

> Where is my God? What hidden place
>   Conceals thee still?
> What covert dare eclipse thy face?
>   Is it thy will?
>
> O let not that of any thing;
>   Let rather brasse,
> Or steel, or mountains be thy ring,
>   And I will passe.
>
> Thy will such an intrenching is,
>   As passeth thought:
> To it all strength, all subtilties
>   Are things of nought.

7. Nuttall, "The Shocking Image," 152.
8. Frost, "The Figure a Poem Makes," 985–986.

> Thy will such a strange distance is,
>   As that to it,
> East and West touch, the poles do kisse,
>   And parallels meet.
>
> Since then my grief must be as large,
>   As is thy space,
> Thy distance from me; see my charge,
>   Lord, see my case.
>
> O take these barres, these lengths away;
>   Turn, and restore me:
> Be not Almightie, let me say,
>   Against, but for me.[9]

Here, Herbert is agonizing (from the Greek word *agon*—"contest," or *agonia*—"struggle") over the possibility that the distance he feels from God is a result not of anything that stands between himself and God, but of the very will of God. In other words, God has chosen to keep Herbert separate from her/him/it. The feeling that this may be the case causes Herbert to cry out to God to use her/his/its sovereign power for him, rather than against him, or else all hope is lost.

This is a deep kind of wrestling with God, and for the reader it occurs in the present moment of the poem—there is no foregone conclusion here. The poem is so successful in articulating the spiritual struggle that we can speculate that Herbert was actually experiencing a sense of separation from God as he composed the poem—it is at least a possibility—so that the spiritual struggle being dramatized is not simply a re-enactment. We cannot know this for certain, but the very fact that the struggle *seems* to be a present concern of the poet as he writes the poem and that the poem *seems* to be the very devotional means through which Herbert engages with his doubt and communicates with God lends power to the poem. It is doubtful (and I think that Frost would have shared my doubt) that a poem as effective as this (and Herbert has many) could have been written toward a foreknown conclusion.

It is true that some 17th-century poems seem to have been written toward a conclusion that was realized before the poem began. This sort of poem might more justly be characterized as a record or imitation of prior spiritual devotion (meditation on a theological mystery, for instance), rather than an act of devotion itself. Some of Donne's "Holy Sonnets" are good examples of this kind of poem. The conclusion of "Holy Sonnet X," for instance, is inherent in first statement of poem. The poem begins with the imperative, "Death be not proud," an order that could not possibly be given by the speaker apart from an already-existing realization of the concluding

9. Herbert, "The Search," 168–170.

theological paradox of the poem: "death, thou shalt die."[10] However, it is my contention that many 17[h]-century poems are examples of exploratory poems—begun in uncertainty of mind and spirit, and themselves representing the devotional process (or at least part of it) through which resolution, or clarity, or simply articulation was achieved.

Although it is, of course, impossible to know, based on the text of the poem alone, to what extent a poet did or did not have the conclusion of the poem in view during the act of composition, we can say this much, at least: Some religious poems (like Herbert's "The Search") dramatize a mental or spiritual struggle; other religious poems (like Donne's "Holy Sonnet X") do not purport to dramatize a current struggle, and instead explain or explicate a struggle that happened prior to the composition of the poem. In the latter case, the entire poem functions as a conclusion; even if there is some dramatization, as there is in Donne's poem (a speaker personifying and addressing death), there is no uncertainty in the rhetoric since the conclusion is foreknown and stated or implied from the beginning. This kind of poem engages the reader the way a sermon or an essay might. On the other hand, the rhetoric of a poem that dramatizes a struggle in the literary "present," as Herbert's poem does, proceeds with uncertainty and thus engages the reader the way a play might. This effect is intensified to the extent that the reader senses that the poet's *composition* of the poem proceeded in uncertainty—not only of the literary or formal outcome of the nascent poem, but also the spiritual outcome of engaging the poem's idea.

Perhaps we should now venture a definition of a devotional poem. In order to do so, we should first define devotional practice. For specifics about 17th-century devotional practice, I refer the reader to Anthony Low's book, *Love's Architecture: Devotional Modes in Seventeenth-century English Poetry*. For our purposes, it will suffice to define devotional practice as any of those practices that an individual uses to relate to the divine. Though 17th-century English poets are of particular interest in this essay, devotional practices are not, of course, limited to 17th-century Europeans; they include all intentional ways of relating to the divine in any culture and at any time. I would suggest the following general categories of devotional practice, which are not specific to time period: confession, petition, praise, and meditation (not only in the sense of quieting one's mind, but also in the opposite sense of mental engagement with theological concepts or mysteries, thus including struggle with uncertainty and doubt).

Having defined devotional practice in very broad terms, we can attempt a definition of a devotional poem: A devotional poem represents the devotional practice of the poet (even if it adopts a persona to do so), and is either a re-enactment of

10. Donne, "Holy Sonnet X," 262.

the devotional practice or is itself (in the process of its composition) part of that practice. Furthermore, theoretically speaking, a poem whose composition was itself part of the devotional practice would be the quintessential devotional poem, and a poem that re-enacts devotional practice, while remaining in the devotional mode, would fall on the periphery of the category. Thus, the devotional mode can usefully be thought of as a spectrum.

III. Devotional Poetry Today

The Metaphysical poets have exerted a particularly strong influence on American poetry, and thus they are the focus of this essay, but so have (and perhaps increasingly so) mystic or ecstatic poets, including Eastern poets such as Rabi'a, Rumi, and Hafiz, as well as Europeans like St. John of the Cross. In fact, we would be remiss to avoid recognizing the mystical or ecstatic poem in any discussion of devotional poetry. The mystical or ecstatic poem can be seen as a sub-category of the devotional poem. However, I would suggest that mystical or ecstatic poems are rarely written by American poets today, and it is primarily in the area of stylistics (rather than mode of composition) that the influence of these poets is evident in contemporary American poetry. On the other hand, it is my contention that some American poets today still write in the broader devotional mode, and that the primary influence on their practice has been 17th-century English poets—an influence that has less to do with stylistics than with the ways in which their devotional poems engage with uncertainty.

The influence of 17th-century English poets transcends stylistics. As Metaphysical poets (if we understand the term to refer to *stylistic* elements), they are inhabitants of a particular time and place; as devotional poets, they inhabit human history, past and future. There are probably no Metaphysical poets today—I certainly know of none—but there are devotional poets. Some poets today occasionally write a poem with a figure that might be considered a metaphysical conceit, for instance, or deal linguistically with paradox in a way that resembles the way the Metaphysicals did, but the stylistic devices of the Metaphysicals are not a lifework for any of our poets. (However, they could be, if anyone were up to the task and inclined toward it—and perhaps, at some point, they *should* be, for the sake of the riches that the practice of the Metaphysical style can make available.) For some, however, poetry is still composed as a devotional practice.

Anthony Low says, "True religious poetry is the product of radical transformation."[11] This gets at what T. S. Eliot identified as the fundamental and vital element in George Herbert's poetry—authenticity:

11. Low, *Love's Architecture*, 237.

> When I claim a place for Herbert among those poets whose work every lover
> of English poetry should read and every student of English poetry should
> study, irrespective of religious belief or unbelief, I am not thinking primarily
> of the exquisite craftmanship, the extraordinary metrical virtuosity, or the ver-
> bal felicities, but of the *content* of the poems which make up *The Temple*. These
> poems form a record of spiritual struggle which should touch the feeling, and
> enlarge the understanding of those readers also who hold no religious belief
> and find themselves unmoved by religious emotion. (italics Eliot's)[12]

If there could be only one criterion for devotional poetry, it would be authenticity of personal religious or spiritual expression. A devotional poem cannot co-opt
religion for non-religious, non-devotional purposes—the poem cannot be ironic in
this sense. A devotional poem must be a *genuine* religious expression or practice,
otherwise it will simply be a commentary on religion from outside of religious experience. Devotional poetry operates from the inside. Furthermore, a devotional poet
does not write out of mere nostalgia for childhood religion or out of the influence
of scriptural and ecclesiastical language, pure and simple. Rather, a devotional poet
engages actively in the pursuit of the divine. Such a poet is literally *devoted* (the
etymology indicates "set apart by a vow") to God.

A further distinction is necessary, because a devout poet does not necessarily
write devotional poetry. Devotional poetry is a distinct category or mode within
the larger categories of "religious" and "spiritual" poetry. As I have mentioned in
the first section, devotional poetry represents the devotional practice of the poet.
A poem may have God, religion, or spirituality as its subject without representing
the poet's devotional practice, so that there are religious and spiritual poets who are
not devotional poets. W. H. Auden is an excellent example; he is clearly a religious
poet, but very rarely a devotional one. Devotional poetry is itself a means of relating
personally with God, rather than simply being a place where theological ideas are
explored, and I think Auden's poetry is the latter. For instance, his long poem *For
the Time Being: A Christmas Oratorio*, like many of his long poems, is presented
from a rhetorical distance, complete with chorus and narrator, so that even though
the subject matter is unerringly religious and the ideas clearly theological, they are
presented with such formal rhetoric as to make them impersonal.

Many of Auden's poems also operate with a tonal irony that is simultaneously
humorous and grave—a marvelous effect, of which he is the master—and that makes
the poems feel less personal than a devotional poem would. Consider the concluding stanzas of "The More Loving One":

12. Eliot, "George Herbert as Religious Poet," 239.

> Admirer as I think I am
> Of stars that do not give a damn,
> I cannot, now I see them, say
> I missed one terribly all day.
>
> Were all stars to disappear or die,
> I should learn to look at an empty sky
> And feel its total dark sublime,
> Though this might take me a little time.[13]

The rhyming couplets in tetrameter lend a "light" quality to this poem, and combined with phrases like "stars that do not give a damn," a humorous effect is achieved. However, the imagined scenario is apocalyptic—the disappearance of all stars from the sky. Just as the scenario is understated, so accordingly is the speaker's response: "I should learn to look at an empty sky / And feel its total dark sublime, / Though this might take me a little time." The confession in the final line strikes the reader as an immense understatement. This kind of irony (in this instance, distance between the tone of the poem and the mood of the speaker, and distance between the statement and its intended meaning) is masterfully wielded in Auden's hand, to great effect. But we can also see how this kind of irony is not suited to the devotional mode, as irony depends for its effect on the "betrayal" of authenticity.

There are some few exceptions in Auden's body of work to the kind of rhetorical and tonal distance noted above—for instance, the poems "The Prophets" and "The Dark Years," which operate without irony and might indeed be considered devotional poems. However, Auden's poetic output from all periods of his life so hinges on irony for its effects that I have chosen not to include his work in this anthology.

Czeslaw Milosz is a fine example of a poet who is usually a religious poet rather than a devotional one, but who has also written some wonderful devotional poems. We do not see the same kind of irony at work in his poems as in Auden's. "An Alcoholic Enters the Gates of Heaven," for instance, from his collection *This*, is addressed directly to God, and it is easy to imagine that the persona of the poem authentically represents the poet himself:

> I pray to you, for I do not know how not to pray.
>
> Because my heart desires you,
> though I do not believe you would cure me.
>
> And so it must be, that those who suffer will continue to suffer,
> praising your name.[14]

---

13. Auden, "The More Loving One," 282.

14. Milosz, "An Alcoholic Enters the Gates of Heaven," *New and Collected*, 734–735.

Uncertainty seems inherent in the above address to God, though it may seem for the reader one step removed from the poet's own uncertainty due to the fact that a persona is speaking. "Prayer," however, from the same collection, seems even more clearly in the poet's own voice:

> Now You are closing down my five senses, slowly,
> And I am an old man lying in darkness.
>
> [. . .]
>
> Liberate me from guilt, real and imagined.
> Give me certainty that I toiled for Your glory.
>
> In the hour of the agony of my death, help me with Your suffering
> Which cannot save the world from pain.[15]

The poet (writing this, I believe, in his eighties) is here describing his ongoing encounter with real uncertainty, and we might speculate that the poem was *composed* in uncertainty as well, which situates it more fully in the devotional mode. Often, however, even when we seem to hear Milosz's own voice, it is primarily an appeal to his fellow humans rather than directly to God, as in "If There Is No God," from the last collection published before his death:

> If there is no God,
> Not everything is permitted to man.
> He is still his brother's keeper
> And he is not permitted to sadden his brother,
> By saying that there is no God.[16]

Much of Milosz's poetry throughout his life was focused on social, historical, and theological issues, almost always religious to one degree or another, but less often devotional.

One of the best examples of a contemporary devotional poet writing in America is Franz Wright. There is a host of recent and living poets who speak about God sporadically or in vague terms, but Franz Wright's persistence in addressing God directly and specifically in his poems is rare, certainly among poets honored by the establishment.[17]

In "Letter," from his collection *Walking to Martha's Vineyard*, Wright writes (in the present tense, you will notice) about a recent religious experience in a church, and then continues the meditation as he recalls walking outside, remarkably changed in attitude:

15. Milosz, "Prayer," *New and Collected*, 742–743.

16. Milosz, "If There Is No God," *Second Space*, 5.

17. Wright was awarded the Pulitzer Prize in 2004.

> When I step outside the ugliness is so shattering
> it has become dear to me, like a retarded
> child, precious to me.
> If only I could tell someone.
> The humiliation I go through
> when I think of my past
> can only be described as grace.
> We are created by being destroyed.[18]

Wright often deals with guilt arising from his long struggle with depression and drug and alcohol abuse, as he does here. In this poem, his experience of guilt has finally been understood as the work of God's grace, and it seems likely that the composition of the poem was itself part of the process of coming to that understanding. Wright is drawn to this kind of paradox, in which something seemingly antagonistic to his faith actually becomes the instrument through which he experiences God, time and again in his meditations. In "Cloudless Snowfall," he says, "thank You for / keeping Your face hidden, I / can hardly bear the beauty of this world."[19] In "Year One," he writes, "Moonlit winter clouds the color of the desperation of wolves. // Proof / of Your existence? There is nothing / but."[20] Wright addresses this paradox in an interview with Ernest Hilbert:

> I think what [George] Herbert is getting at ([Gerard Manley] Hopkins is marvelous at this, too) is that our suffering is the terrible and only teacher—Kierkegaard said famously suffering is the characteristic of God's love—and I think everyone senses that failure and brokenness and loneliness cause us to perceive us as God might, as naked and ignorant and blind. Our suffering may be the real form love takes, but we also know that at the end of it waits infinite peace and radiance, that has been my experience anyway. Why things are arranged this way, who knows—pretty soon we are all going to find out.[21]

Wright believes in the grace of God being mediated through suffering to such an extent that he is able to write, "Fill me with love for the *truly* afflicted / that hopeless love, if need be / make me one of them again."[22] And similarly, in "The Process," he writes about his experience of unpredictable and inexplicable joy, as well as its inverse—unpredictable and inexplicable agony. The movement of the poem is into an attitude of submission to and acceptance of God's will, even if it requires his relapse into "the

---

18. Wright, "Letter," *Walking to Martha's Vineyard*, 38–39.

19. Wright, "Cloudless Snowfall," *Walking to Martha's Vineyard*, 24.

20. Wright, "Year One," *Walking to Martha's Vineyard*, 3.

21. Hilbert, "The Secret Glory."

22. Wright, "Why is the Winter Light," *God's Silence*, 90–91.

long black killing years" that "can always come again // according to Your will." He concludes, "this time / I will not whine, I will obey // and be / (forever) / still."[23]

In his interview with Hilbert, Wright seems to indicate that the composition of his poems is very much a devotional process. He says, "I would say that the one and only reward of writing is the experience of writing—if you take it seriously, technically and spiritually—the experience, that secret glory, itself."[24] And in another interview, with Ilya Kaminsky and Katherine Towler, he says, "Writing is listening. Religious experience is silent listening and waiting. I have always been able to tell whether something I am writing is genuinely an expression of revelation or if it's just me exercising my intellect. I can feel the difference, see it and taste it, but I don't know how I can do that."[25] In "Kyrie," a poem from Wright's collection *Wheeling Motel*, he writes, "he was legibly told what to say and he wrote // with mounting excitement and pleasure . . . ."[26] The "he" of this poem is certainly the poet, discovering what it is he will write as he writes it—as it is dictated to him from outside. This is the "listening" and "revelation" Wright spoke of in his interview.

In Wright's poem "The Only Animal," he writes,

> this morning
> I stood once again
> in this world, the garden
> ark and vacant
> tomb of what
> I can't imagine,
> between twin eternities,
> some sort of wings,
> more or less equidistantly
> exiled from both,
> hovering in the dreaming called
> being awake, where
> You gave me
> in secret one thing
> to perceive, the
> tall blue starry
> strangeness of being
> here at all.[27]

---

23. Wright, "The Process," *God's Silence*, 135.
24. Hilbert, "The Secret Glory: An Interview with Franz Wright."
25. Kaminsky and Towler, "A Conversation with Franz Wright."
26. Wright, "Kyrie," *Wheeling Motel*, 7.
27. Wright, "The Only Animal," *Walking to Martha's Vineyard*, 73–75.

The "strangeness of being" is an enduring uncertainty about which the poet meditates, presumably both in moments like the one described in the poem and through the very composition of this and other poems.

In Wright's poetry, uncertainty is often the impetus for the writing, and the writing is a means of engaging the uncertainty in an act of devotion (a meditation, often explicitly addressed to God). These are the poems of Wright's that are most fully devotional. He does, however, have many poems that seem to record devotional experiences rather than enact them in their composition; these poems remain in the devotional mode, though more peripherally than poems like "The Only Animal." But in general, Wright's poetry is devotional in the truest sense of the word—not only does it record religious experience and devotional practice, but it is often itself part of that devotional practice, which for Wright involves "listening" and "revelation."

But Wright is not alone. The 77 poets in this anthology demonstrate that the devotional mode is not a relic of a particular time period or cultural paradigm, but is rather a vital, living artistic mode. I chose to include poets who were alive in 1950 and afterward for this very purpose. From now-canonical voices like T. S. Eliot and Theodore Roethke which resound with authority, to the deep interiority of poets like Patrice de la Tour du Pin and R. S. Thomas; from the monastic perspectives of Madeline DeFrees and Thomas Merton, to worldly-wise voices like Denise Levertov and Mary Karr; from the thoughtful songwriters Leonard Cohen and Sufjan Stevens, to the dramatic monologues of Andrew Hudgins, Maurice Manning, and Ashley Anna McHugh; from Amit Majmudar's mystical Islamic setting of *Paradise Lost*, to Bruce Beasley's fragmented and searching self-portrait; from Jane Hirshfield's intuition of an otherness, to the Orthodox meditations of Scott Cairns; from well-known figures like Charles Wright, Louise Glück, Agha Shahid Ali, and Mark Jarman, to lesser-known, extraordinary poets like Judy Little, Stella Vinitchi Radulescu, Philip Metres, and Malachi Black; from 1888 to 1991—these poets testify to the ongoing importance of the devotional mode in poetry.

These poets are not Metaphysical poets, but they are devotional ones in the long tradition of the Old Testament psalmists, medieval mystical poets, 17th-century English poets, and later devotional poets like Gerard Manley Hopkins and Rainer Maria Rilke. Together, the poets included in this anthology demonstrate that stylistics are constantly changing in poetry, but devotion itself endures, with the power to, in Eliot's phrase, "touch the feeling, and enlarge the understanding."

Bibliography

Auden, W. H. *Collected Shorter Poems: 1927–1957*. New York: Random House, 1966.

Donne, John. *The Complete Poetry and Selected Prose of John Donne*, edited by Charles M. Coffin. New York: The Modern Library, 2001.

Eliot, T. S. "George Herbert as Religious Poet." In *George Herbert and the Seventeenth-century Religious Poets*, edited by Mario A. di Cesare. New York: W. W. Norton, 1978.

Frost, Robert. "The Figure a Poem Makes." In *The Norton Anthology of Modern and Contemporary Poetry* (Third Edition), edited by Jahan Ramazani et al. New York: W. W. Norton, 2003.

Herbert, George. *The English Poems of George Herbert*, edited by C. A. Patrides. London: J. M. Dent & Sons, 1974.

Hilbert, Ernest. "The Secret Glory: An Interview with Franz Wright." *Contemporary Poetry Review* (2006). Online: http://www.cprw.com/Hilbert/wright.htm. Accessed April 2, 2009.

Kaminsky, Ilya and Katherine Towler. "A Conversation with Franz Wright." *Image* 51 (Fall, 2006). Online: http://poems.com/special_features/prose/essay_wright.php. Accessed April 2, 2009.

Low, Anthony. *Love's Architecture: Devotional Modes in Seventeenth-century English Poetry*. New York: New York University Press, 1978.

———. "Metaphysical Poets and Devotional Poets." In *George Herbert and the Seventeenth-century Religious Poets*, edited by Mario A. di Cesare. New York: W. W. Norton, 1978.

Milosz, Czeslaw. *New and Collected Poems: 1931–2001*. New York: Ecco, 2001.

———. *Second Space*. New York: Ecco, 2004.

Nuttall, A. D. "The Shocking Image." In *The Metaphysical Poets*, edited by Frank Kermode. New York: Fawcett, 1969.

Wright, Franz. *God's Silence*. New York: Alfred A. Knopf, 2006.

———. *Walking to Martha's Vineyard*. New York: Alfred A. Knopf, 2004.

———. *Wheeling Motel*. New York: Alfred A. Knopf, 2009.

A Note on the Selection

AN ANTHOLOGY OF THIS kind could not pretend to be exhaustive, and the selection of poets and poems in this volume certainly demonstrates the editor's aesthetic preferences. There are poets whose work fits within the devotional mode (as discussed in the introduction to this volume) that I chose to exclude for aesthetic reasons. I believe that aesthetic vision and discernment are vital aspects of the role of an editor. Another editor might have chosen differently, and that is as it should be.

Also, undoubtedly there are poets of whom I am ignorant who would have been included had I encountered their work. Be that as it may, I believe that my selection represents the diversity and excellence to be found within the devotional mode in this era.

Finally, the reader will notice that although my focus in this volume is on recent literature written in the United States, I have also included some work from other countries that is either widely read in the U.S. or that I believe should be more widely read here.

The work included in this anthology continues to move and challenge me. I trust it will do so for the reader as well.

Luke Hankins

Poems of Devotion

T. S. Eliot
(1888–1965)

FROM *FOUR QUARTETS*

from "East Coker"

IV.

The wounded surgeon plies the steel
That questions the distempered part;
Beneath the bleeding hands we feel
The sharp compassion of the healer's art
Resolving the enigma of the fever chart.

    Our only health is the disease
If we obey the dying nurse
Whose constant care is not to please
But to remind of our, and Adam's curse,
And that, to be restored, our sickness must grow worse.

    The whole earth is our hospital
Endowed by the ruined millionaire,
Wherein, if we do well, we shall
Die of the absolute paternal care
That will not leave us, but prevents us everywhere.

    The chill ascends from feet to knees,
The fever sings in mental wires.
If to be warmed, then I must freeze
And quake in frigid purgatorial fires
Of which the flame is roses, and the smoke is briars.

    The dripping blood our only drink,
The bloody flesh our only food:
In spite of which we like to think
That we are sound, substantial flesh and blood—
Again, in spite of that, we call this Friday good.

T. S. Eliot

from "Little Gidding"

V.

What we call the beginning is often the end
And to make an end is to make a beginning.
The end is where we start from. And every phrase
And sentence that is right (where every word is at home,
Taking its place to support the others,
The word neither diffident nor ostentatious,
An easy commerce of the old and the new,
The common word exact without vulgarity,
The formal word precise but not pedantic,
The complete consort dancing together)
Every phrase and every sentence is an end and a beginning,
Every poem an epitaph. And any action
Is a step to the block, to the fire, down the sea's throat
Or to an illegible stone: and that is where we start.
We die with the dying:
See, they depart, and we go with them.
We are born with the dead:
See, they return, and bring us with them.
The moment of the rose and the moment of the yew-tree
Are of equal duration. A people without history
Is not redeemed from time, for history is a pattern
Of timeless moments. So, while the light fails
On a winter's afternoon, in a secluded chapel
History is now and England.
With the drawing of this Love and the voice of this
        Calling

        We shall not cease from exploration
And the end of all our exploring
Will be to arrive where we started
And know the place for the first time.
Through the unknown, remembered gate
When the last of earth left to discover
Is that which was the beginning;
At the source of the longest river
The voice of the hidden waterfall
And the children in the apple-tree
Not known, because not looked for
But heard, half-heard, in the stillness
Between two waves of the sea.
Quick now, here, now, always—
A condition of complete simplicity
(Costing not less than everything)

T. S. Eliot

And all shall be well and
All manner of thing shall be well
When the tongues of flame are in-folded
Into the crowned knot of fire
And the fire and the rose are one.

E. E. Cummings
(1894–1962)

[I THANK YOU GOD FOR MOST THIS AMAZING]

i thank You God for most this amazing
day:for the leaping greenly spirits of trees
and a blue true dream of sky;and for everything
which is natural which is infinite which is yes

(i who have died am alive again today,
and this is the sun's birthday;this is the birth
day of life and of love and wings:and of the gay
great happening illimitably earth)

how should tasting touching hearing seeing
breathing any—lifted from the no
of all nothing—human merely being
doubt unimaginable You?

(now the ears of my ears awake and
now the eyes of my eyes are opened)

Robert Penn Warren
(1905–1989)

A WAY TO LOVE GOD

Here is the shadow of truth, for only the shadow is true.
And the line where the incoming swell from the sunset Pacific
First leans and staggers to break will tell all you need to know
About submarine geography, and your father's death rattle
Provides all biographical data required for the *Who's Who* of the dead.

I cannot recall what I started to tell you, but at least
I can say how night-long I have lain under stars and
Heard mountains moan in their sleep. By daylight,
They remember nothing, and go about their lawful occasions
Of not going anywhere except in slow disintegration. At night
They remember, however, that there is something they cannot remember,
So moan. Theirs is the perfected pain of conscience, that
Of forgetting the crime, and I hope you have not suffered it. I have.

I do not recall what had burdened my tongue, but urge you
To think on the slug's white belly, how sick-slick and soft,
On the hairiness of stars, silver, silver, while the silence
Blows like wind by, and on the sea's virgin bosom unveiled
To give suck to the wavering serpent of the moon; and,
In the distance, in *plaza, piazza, place, platz*, and square,
Boot heels, like history being born, on cobbles bang.

Everything seems an echo of something else.

And when, by the hair, the headsman held up the head
Of Mary of Scots, the lips kept on moving,
But without sound. The lips,
They were trying to say something very important.

But I had forgotten to mention an upland
Of wind-tortured stone white in darkness, and tall, but when
No wind, mist gathers, and once on the Sarré at midnight,
I watched the sheep huddling. Their eyes
Stared into nothingness. In that mist-diffused light their eyes
Were stupid and round like the eyes of fat fish in muddy water,
Or of a scholar who has lost faith in his calling.

Robert Penn Warren

Their jaws did not move. Shreds
Of dry grass, gray in gray mist-light, hung
From the side of a jaw, unmoving.

You would think that nothing would ever again happen.

That may be a way to love God.

Theodore Roethke
(1908–1963)

IN A DARK TIME

In a dark time, the eye begins to see,
I meet my shadow in the deepening shade;
I hear my echo in the echoing wood—
A lord of nature weeping to a tree.
I live between the heron and the wren,
Beasts of the hill and serpents of the den.

What's madness but nobility of soul
At odds with circumstance? The day's on fire!
I know the purity of pure despair,
My shadow pinned against a sweating wall.
That place among the rocks—is it a cave,
Or winding path? The edge is what I have.

A steady storm of correspondences!
A night flowing with birds, a ragged moon,
And in broad day the midnight come again!
A man goes far to find out what he is—
Death of the self in a long, tearless night,
All natural shapes blazing unnatural light.

Dark, dark my light, and darker my desire.
My soul, like some heat-maddened summer fly,
Keeps buzzing at the sill. Which I is *I*?
A fallen man, I climb out of my fear.
The mind enters itself, and God the mind,
And one is One, free in the tearing wind.

M. Vasalis
(1909–1998)

SIMULTANEITY

Six in the evening, in the kitchen

The little dog with pricked-up ears,
the potatoes boiling on the stove,
the wooden tick of the clock—the sky
far and gray-blue and the jewelweeds,
tall as people. The pasture
with uneven tussocks and their shadows,
like drawings in a cave. And the knifelike light
that burns through the leaves, a glittering mystery.
And I—another creature, watching it.
It blends together and it doesn't change.
Oh Lord. I feel that something ought
to be made clear to me. That I've been granted time,
and yet, however overwhelmed I am,
something is missing that would help me say: this order,
however slipshod it may be: I see it, I'm awakened.
Forgive my being deaf and being blind,
and hold me in your greatness—I am small,
but have, as well, too many tentacles
that grope in the different-being Being.

Translated from the Dutch by Fred Lessing and David Young

Patrice de la Tour du Pin
(1911–1975)

Psalm 6

Then I came to dream of writing
the great prayer of our time . . .

This ambition plagues me constantly:
I could never have the right to such a voice.

I draw, of course, from the choir of voices in my soul,
voices that come to me through blood or friendship,

chance cries and similar calls for grace,
even echoes of those I've barely encountered.

I assemble an interior liturgy in this way,
by finding the great number who reside in me.

If my dream is laughable, Lord,
extinguish it, for it consumes me.

It guides me in what I seek:
could poetry be a kind of grace?

I hold on to this lovely hope
more tenacious at times than my demons.

But human thirst infiltrates it as well:
my most intimate liturgy would like to be the most intimate of all.

One must be able to hear the cry of others, to do nothing but
empty the self for the sake of a common call.

To hear in the voices of others your love cry and your lament:
so I go silent: you hold me.

Translated from the French by Jennifer Grotz

Patrice de la Tour du Pin

Psalm 25

You allotted me too much happiness, my God!
How will I answer for this before you?

My portion of suffering is trivial
and I don't have the heart to ask you to increase it.

You allotted me a vocation of speaking,
but that doesn't suffice.

In this vocation I glean pain from the world:
but that's less difficult than being myself prey to pain!

I empty myself so that life and word will align,
I exhaust myself to locate them in the same heart.

But my sacrifice insists its way toward joy—
it hardly leads me to relinquish my happiness.

I look at your Christ and am terrified.
My privileges are too heavy to bear.

It's not being happy that eats away at me,
but the anguish of the scandal of even speaking about the Lord.

One could say: no, you are not carrying his sign,
you are burying yourself so as not to be hurt outside!

But me, I can do nothing but believe in your grace,
and beneath my happiness shudders a dark joy.

Translated from the French by Jennifer Grotz

Psalm 41

My God, I know only my debt,
all my life carried in debt—
and you who repay it in a word!

Forgive me my shamelessness:
you who have hedged me in from all directions at once,
deliver me in time for your day of rest.

Set the night sky back in motion,
reweave the constellations
into a scaffold for your praise.

On that day when you judge
the taste of my joy with your lips,
my sorrow at your Passion,

will you be able to say: "Here is a man
who valued me
over thirty radiant ideas"?

Translated from the French by Jennifer Grotz

PSALM 52

To the one who waits for me where the desert ends,
and sardonic, mocking, interrogates me about manna:
Without it, would I be here, with an open book?

Remember that I was undertaking my quest
for him, for me, for God also . . . remember:
can't one search for joy?

But everything gets muddled in my head . . .
death suspended from the head,
who could actually run after joy?

Every way leads to agony, of course!
The future is clear:
little by little all the dreams are broken.

So where should I have gone instead?
You showed me your doorway to the future,
perhaps imprudently, my God!

It's you who lead me ahead into the desert.
Ahead? Yes, of course, it wasn't yet time
for me to surrender my flesh.

Ahead? But you alone can lead my flesh forward!
Yes, of course, I understood nothing, I was throwing myself
against your wind that murmured:

Patrice de la Tour du Pin

"Come, it's still a time of crusade on earth,
not to the places of unbelievers from another time,
but to the seal of death man carries inside himself.

"Come: don't look any longer for my tomb on earth."
Ah! It takes so much time to see oneself as a tomb
and how slow the age of the Church is to break it!

Somehow, I lived through this exodus.
Perhaps imprudently, I even described it . . . .
What? Did I keep my book? Here it is.

Translated from the French by Jennifer Grotz

Czeslaw Milosz
(1911–2004)

AN ALCOHOLIC ENTERS THE GATES OF HEAVEN

What kind of man I was to be you've known since the beginning,
since the beginning of every creature.

It must be horrible to be aware, simultaneously,
of what is, what was,
and what will be.

I began my life confident and happy,
certain that the Sun rose every day for me
and that flowers opened for me every morning.
I ran all day in an enchanted garden.

Not suspecting that you had picked me from the Book of Genes
for another experiment altogether.
As if there were not proof enough
that free will is useless against destiny.

Under your amused glance I suffered
like a caterpillar impaled on the spike of a blackthorn.
The terror of the world opened itself to me.

Could I have avoided escape into illusion?
Into a liquor which stopped the chattering of teeth
and melted the burning ball in my breast
and made me think I could live like others?

I realized I was wandering from hope to hope
and I asked you, All Knowing, why you torture me.
Is it a trial like Job's,[1] so that I call faith a phantom
and say: You are not, nor do your verdicts exist,
and the earth is ruled by accident?

Who can contemplate
simultaneous, a-billion-times-multiplied pain?

It seems to me that people who cannot believe in you
deserve your praise.

1. See the biblical book of Job.

But perhaps because you were overwhelmed by pity,
you descended to the earth
to experience the condition of mortal creatures.

Bore the pain of crucifixion for a sin, but committed by whom?

I pray to you, for I do not know how not to pray.

Because my heart desires you,
though I do not believe you would cure me.

And so it must be, that those who suffer will continue to suffer,
praising your name.

Translated from the Polish by Czeslaw Milosz and Robert Hass

PRAYER

Approaching ninety, and still with a hope
That I could tell it, say it, blurt it out.

If not before people, at least before You,
Who nourished me with honey and wormwood.

I am ashamed, for I must believe you protected me,
As if I had for You some particular merit.

I was like those in the gulags[2] who fashioned a cross from twigs
And prayed to it at night in the barracks.

I made a plea and You deigned to answer it,
So that I could see how unreasonable it was.

But when out of pity for others I begged a miracle,
The sky and the earth were silent, as always.

Morally suspect because of my belief in You,
I admired unbelievers for their simple persistence.

What sort of adorer of Majesty am I,
If I consider religion good only for the weak like myself?

---

2. *gulags*: Soviet forced-labor camps.

The least-normal person in Father Chomski's class,
I had already fixed my sights on the swirling vortex of a destiny.

Now You are closing down my five senses, slowly,
And I am an old man lying in darkness.

Delivered to that thing which has oppressed me
So that I always ran forward, composing poems.

Liberate me from guilt, real and imagined.
Give me certainty that I toiled for Your glory.

In the hour of the agony of death, help me with Your suffering
Which cannot save the world from pain.

Translated from the Polish by Czeslaw Milosz and Robert Hass

William Everson (Brother Antoninus)
(1912–1994)

STORM-SURGE

Christmas Eve, night of nights, and Big Creek
Is on the move. At the equinox
Tempting rains toyed with us, teasing, and offshore at sea,
Beyond the slant sandbar blocking the rivermouth,
The great grey salmon skulked in the trough, dreaming the long
Genetic dream, plasmatic slumber of the unfulfilled,
Awaiting the moment of the forth-showing,
The river-tongue in the sea's vulva,
The strength in the slot.

        First incremental showers
Flushed dead vegetation, cathartic,
Purging the veins of the cleft mountain.
Then a month of drought reimposed itself,
The turbid summer's condign sterility
Drying the glades, sucking the flow back into the hills,
As if the mountain begrudged what it gave, called back its gifts,
Summoning them home, the high largess
Repentant of its grace.

        Advent[3] broke dry,
December harsh on the hills, no sign of cloud
On the steely horizon. But solstice
Brought respite: a northwest flurry
Shook the last limbs bare, the drum of hailstones
Rattling the shingles under riddled cloud.
Then wind swung south and nimbus struck,
One thousand-mile storm enveloping the coast,
Forty-eight hours of vertical rain, water falling
Like the splurge of God, the squandering of heaven—
As if forever on the mountains and the draws,
As if forever on the river-forks and creeks,
As if forever on the vast watershed, its sheer
Declivities, its seaward-pitching slides,
Thirst-shrunken slopes of the parched ridges.

---

3. *Advent*: The Christian season leading up to Christmas in anticipation of the birth of Christ.

And I lean in the dark, the harsh
Pulsation of night, Big Creek
Gorged in torrent, hearing its logs
Hit those boulders, chute that flood,
Batter their weight to the sandbar
And the sea, ripping a channel
Out to the future, the space beyond time,
On the eve of the coming, when Christ,
The principle in the purpose,
Splits the womb in his shudder of birth.

R. S. Thomas
(1913–2000)

KNEELING

Moments of great calm,
Kneeling before an altar
Of wood in a stone church
In summer, waiting for the God
To speak; the air a staircase
For silence; the sun's light
Ringing me, as though I acted
A great rôle. And the audiences
Still; all that close throng
Of spirits waiting, as I,
For the message.
            Prompt me, God;
But not yet. When I speak,
Though it be you who speak
Through me, something is lost.
The meaning is in the waiting.

THRESHOLD

I emerge from the mind's
cave into the worse darkness
outside, where things pass and
the Lord is in none of them.

I have heard the still, small voice
and it was that of the bacteria
demolishing my cosmos. I
have lingered too long on

this threshold, but where can I go?
To look back is to lose the soul
I was leading upwards towards
the light. To look forward? Ah,

what balance is needed at
the edges of such an abyss.
I am alone on the surface
of a turning planet. What

to do but, like Michelangelo's
Adam, put my hand
out into unknown space,
hoping for the reciprocating touch?

John Berryman
(1914–1972)

from "Eleven Addresses to the Lord"

9

Surprise me on some ordinary day
with a blessing gratuitous. Even I've done good
beyond their expectations. What count we then
upon Your bounty?

Interminable: an old theologian
asserts that even to say You exist is misleading.
Uh-huh. I buy that Second-century fellow.
I press his withered glorifying hand.

You certainly do not as I exist,
impersonating as well the meteorite
& flaring in your sun your waterfall
or blind in caves pallid fishes.

Bear in mind me, Who have forgotten nothing,
& Who continues. I may not foreknow
& fail much to remember. You sustain
imperial desuetudes,[4] at the kerb a widow.

---

4. *desuetude*: Something no longer in use or no longer practiced.

William Stafford
(1914–1993)

["ARE YOU MR. WILLIAM STAFFORD?"]⁵

"Are you Mr. William Stafford?"
"Yes, but . . . ."

Well, it was yesterday.
Sunlight used to follow my hand.
And that's when the strange siren-like sound flooded
over the horizon and rushed through the streets of our town.
That's when sunlight came from behind
a rock and began to follow my hand.

"It's for the best," my mother said—"Nothing can
ever be wrong for anyone truly good."
So later the sun settled back and the sound
faded and was gone. All along the streets every
house waited, white, blue, gray; trees
were still trying to arch as far as they could.

You can't tell when strange things with meaning
will happen. I'm [still] here writing it down
just the way it was. "You don't have to
prove anything," my mother said. "Just be ready
for what God sends." I listened and put my hand
out in the sun again. It was all easy.

Well, it was yesterday. And the sun came,
Why
It came.

<hr>

5. This is the final poem William Stafford wrote, written on August 28, 1993, the day before his death. Note that the word "[still]"—including the hard brackets—in line 16 appears in the original handwritten manuscript, probably because Stafford was debating whether to include the word.

Thomas Merton
(1915–1968)

EVENING: ZERO WEATHER

Now the lone world is streaky as a wall of marble
With veins of clear and frozen snow.
There is no bird-song there, no hare's track
No badger working in the russet grass:
All the bare fields are silent as eternity.

And the whole herd is home in the long barn.
The brothers come, with hoods about their faces,
Following their plumes of breath
Lugging the gleaming buckets one by one.

This was a day when shovels would have struck
Full flakes of fire out of the land like rock:
And ground cries out like iron beneath our boots

When all the monks come in with eyes as clean as the cold sky
And axes under their arms,
Still paying out *Ave Marias*
With rosaries between their bleeding fingers.

We shake the chips out of our robes outside the door
And go to hide in cowls as deep as clouds,
Bowing our shoulders in the church's shadow, lean and whipped,
To wait upon your Vespers, Mother of God!

And we have eyes no more for the dark pillars or the freezing windows,
Ears for the rumorous cloister or the chimes of time above our heads:
For we are sunken in the summer of our adoration,
And plunge, down, down into the fathoms of our secret joy
That swims with indefinable fire.
And we will never see the copper sunset
Linger a moment, like an echo, on the frozen hill
Then suddenly die an hour before the Angelus.

For we have found our Christ, our August
Here in the zero days before Lent—[6]
We are already binding up our sheaves of harvest

6. *Lent*: In the Catholic Church, a 40-day period (excluding Sundays) of fasting and penance in preparation for Easter (the celebration of the resurrection of Christ).

Beating the lazy liturgy, going up with exultation
Even on the eve of our Ash Wednesday,[7]
And entering our blazing heaven by the doors of the Assumption![8]

O Sweet Irrational Worship

Wind and a bobwhite[9]
And the afternoon sun.

By ceasing to question the sun
I have become light,

Bird and wind.

My leaves sing.

I am earth, earth

All these lighted things
Grow from my heart.

A tall, spare pine
Stands like the initial of my first
Name when I had one.

When I had a spirit,
When I was on fire
When this valley was
Made out of fresh air
You spoke my name
In naming Your silence:
O sweet, irrational worship!

I am earth, earth
My heart's love
Bursts with hay and flowers.
I am a lake of blue air
In which my own appointed place

7. *Ash Wednesday*: In the Catholic Church, this day marks the beginning of Lent and is observed in a service in which the priest marks a cross on the foreheads of worshippers with ashes.

8. *Assumption:* In the Catholic Church, the celebration of the bodily ascension of the Virgin Mary into heaven.

9. *bobwhite*: A kind of quail.

Thomas Merton

Field and valley
Stand reflected.

I am earth, earth

Out of my grass heart
Rises the bobwhite.

Out of my nameless weeds
His foolish worship.

Madeline DeFrees
(b. 1919)

SKID ROW[10]

Out of the depths have I cried, O Lord,
Where the lean heart preys on the hardened crust,
Where short wicks falter on candle-hopes
And winter whips at a patchwork trust.

From darkened doorways no welcome shines,
No promise waits up the broken stair,
And the coin that summons the night with wine
Buys a morning of sick despair.

Out of the depths have I cried in vain
And the still streets echo my lonely calls;
All the long night in the moaning wind
The bruised reed breaks and the sparrow falls.

PSALM FOR A NEW NUN[11]

My life was rescued like a bird from the fowler's snare.
It comes back singing tonight in my loosened hair

as I bend to the mirror in this contracted room
lit by the electric music of the comb.

With hair cropped close as a boy's, contained in a coif,
I let years make me forget what I had cut off.

Now the glass cannot compass my dark halo
and the frame censors the dense life it cannot follow.

Like strength restored in the temple this sweetness wells
quietly into tissues of abandoned cells;

better by as much as it is better to be
a woman, I feel this gradual urgency

10. *skid row*: An idiomatic term for an impoverished and dilapidated urban area.

11. In reference to the lines in italics, see Psalms 91:3, 121:2, and 124:7 & 8.

till the comb snaps, the mirror widens, and the walls recede.
With head uncovered I am no longer afraid.

Broken is the snare and I am freed.
My help is in the name of the Lord who made
heaven and earth. Yes, earth.

FROM THE *LIGHT STATION* ON *TILLAMOOK ROCK*

XII. Geography as Warning

The wildcat drilling started in 1919, the year
of my birth. The legend grows. Where
then, was Lion Rock, two feet
offshore, the name a halo and the claws
retracted as if something more could be expected
of the sleeping form
the ocean gives a voice? An active coastline—
land, risen; or sea level, dropped: swales,
breaker bars and scarps.[12] The fracture
zones. At the bottom of a bay
lies the Millicoma floodplain, Morphic river-
tongues in thousands, whose meaning
no one knows.

          The Seaside Nat, circa 1928.
In the heated pool I stroked away ocean shock,
my heart developing a slight
murmur. Even then Pacific waters meant a mutual
embrace. Rockaway at ten, starfish
clinging to the rocks we balanced on. Black gym
bloomers, sailor blouse, knit beret: I
am the younger version of those boaters, argyles
and golf knickers; women in short
skirts and slingback shoes, there on the putting
green.

          Later, Agate Beach, white-ribbon stone
cut and polished for my first ring.
Newport and rhododendron. Bandon in April, wind
an evil force. Abandoned by a traveling
superior who planned this Arctic curse, an early
spring picnic, we shivered
by a three-foot wall until, at five, our driver

12. *scarps*: Steep cliffs formed by faulting or fracturing of the earth's crust.

back, we were delivered
to our winter home.

           Gearhart, our isolated
summer place. Old nuns and sickly younger ones
kept busy those strong enough to work.
Mid-forties, then, we sneaked in twenties bathing
suits, out the back door, over the hill,
to reappear as tourists, believing they couldn't
tell. Medieval costumes, a giveaway,
not to mention white arms and whiter legs.
Limbs, an old nun called them. "I'd like a
limb of lamb," on Saturday.

           Next, Lincoln City:
holiday on the fringe. Writing up a storm
through that perfect week, the disk
mending slowly. Years after, balanced between
out and in, and ready for the perfect
ending, a trip to Neah Bay, I saw our friend,
Skipper, slam the car door on his index
finger and sweated out the day. The old wounds
open like anemones. We
pray them shut.

           The names float like buoys of
every kind—lighted whistle, spar
buoy, can, nun buoy, bell, and we are on our
knees again, map spread out like comics:

           Cape
Sebastian where the arrows fell. *O all ye canny*
mariners and martyrs, Pray for us. O
all ye terrors lurking off the coast, Pray
for us. O all ye inland patrons of the lost,
Ora pro nobis.[13]

           Cape Lookout mapped as a dagger,
Pray for us. Cape Perpetua
gored by wild beasts, *Pray for us.* Cape Shoal-
water, Cape Foulweather, Destruction
Island, Camp Castaway, *Spare us*
O Lord.

13. *Ora pro nobis*: (Latin) "Pray for us."

Madeline DeFrees

   Cannibal Mountain, Butcherknife Creek,
Turnagain Arm, Quicksand Bay, Devils
Churn, Spouting Horn, Boiler Bay, *Turn not away*
Your Face from us, Hear us, O Lord,
Have mercy.

    The oceanic floor: anatomy becomes
familiar as the forms we walk inside.
Wrecks containing treasure, the flowering skull.

János Pilinszky
(1921–1981)

COMPLAINT

Buried beneath live stars
in the mud of nights
do you hear my dumbness?
as if a skyfull of birds were approaching.

I keep up this wordless appeal.
Will you ever disinter me
from the unending silence
under your foreign skies?

Does my complaint reach you?
Is my siege to no purpose?
All around me glitter
reefs of fear.

Only let me trust you, God.
I want your nearness so much,
shivering
makes the love of loves even fierier.

Bury me in your embrace.
Do not give me to the frost.
Even if my air is used up
my calling will not tire.

Be the bliss of my trembling
like a tree's leaves:
give a name, give a beautiful name
a pillow to this disintegration.

Translated from the Hungarian by Ted Hughes and János Csokits

Richard Wilbur
(b. 1921)

Love Calls Us to the Things of This World

The eyes open to a cry of pulleys,
And spirited from sleep, the astounded soul
Hangs for a moment bodiless and simple
As false dawn.
                    Outside the open window
The morning air is all awash with angels.

Some are in bed-sheets, some are in blouses,
Some are in smocks: but truly there they are.
Now they are rising together in calm swells
Of halcyon feeling, filling whatever they wear
With the deep joy of their impersonal breathing;

Now they are flying in place, conveying
The terrible speed of their omnipresence, moving
And staying like white water; and now of a sudden
They swoon down into so rapt a quiet
That nobody seems to be there.
                          The soul shrinks

From all that it is about to remember,
From the punctual rape of every blessèd day,
And cries,
          "Oh, let there be nothing on earth but laundry,
Nothing but rosy hands in the rising steam
And clear dances done in the sight of heaven."

Yet, as the sun acknowledges
With a warm look the world's hunks and colors,
The soul descends once more in bitter love
To accept the waking body, saying now
In a changed voice as the man yawns and rises,
          "Bring them down from their ruddy gallows;
Let there be clean linen for the backs of thieves;
Let lovers go fresh and sweet to be undone,
And the heaviest nuns walk in a pure floating
Of dark habits,
                  keeping their difficult balance."

Richard Wilbur

"A World Without Objects is a Sensible Emptiness"[14]

The tall camels of the spirit
Steer for their deserts, passing the last groves loud
With the sawmill shrill of the locust, to the whole honey of the arid
Sun. They are slow, proud,

And move with a stilted stride
To the land of sheer horizon, hunting Traherne's
Sensible emptiness, there where the brain's lantern-slide
Revels in vast returns.

O connoisseurs of thirst,
Beasts of my soul who long to learn to drink
Of pure mirage, those prosperous islands are accurst
That shimmer on the brink

Of absence; auras, lustres,
And all shinings need to be shaped and borne.
Think of those painted saints, capped by the early masters
With bright, jauntily worn

Aureate plates, or even
Merry-go-round rings. Turn, O turn
From the fine sleights of the sand, from the long empty oven
Where flames in flamings burn,

Back to the trees arrayed
In bursts of glare, to the halo-dialing run
Of the country creeks, and the hills' bracken tiaras made
Gold in the sunken sun,

Wisely watch for the sight
Of the supernova burgeoning over the barn,[15]
Lampshine blurred in the steam of beasts, the spirit's right
Oasis, light incarnate.

14. See Thomas Traherne's (1637–1674) "The Second Century," meditation 65, from *Centuries of Meditations*.

15. A reference to the biblical story of the star that led the magi to the Christ child.

Anthony Hecht
(1923–2004)

FROM "RITES AND CEREMONIES"

I. The Room

Father, Adonoi,[16] author of all things,
      of the three states,
the soft light on the barn at dawn,
      a wind that sings
in the bracken, fire in iron grates,
      the ram's horn,
Furnisher, hinger of heaven, who bound
      the lovely Pleiades,
entered the perfect treasuries of the snow,
      established the round
course of the world, birth, death and disease,
      and caused to grow
veins, brain, bones in me, to breathe and sing
      fashioned me air,
Lord, who, governing cloud and waterspout,
      O my King,
held me alive till this my forty-third year—
      in whom we doubt—
Who was that child of whom they tell
      in lauds and threnes?[17]
whose holy name all shall pronounce
      Emmanuel,
which being interpreted means,
      "Gott mit uns"?[18]

I saw it on their belts. A young one, dead,
Left there on purpose to get us used to the sight
When we first moved in. Helmet spilled off, head
Blond and boyish and bloody. I was scared that night.
And the sign was there,
The sign of the child, the grave, worship and loss,
Gunpowder heavy as pollen in winter air,
An Iron Cross.

16. *Adonoi*: (Hebrew; usually anglicized as *Adonai*) "Lord."

17. *threne*: A lamentation or dirge.

18. *Emmanuel* is a name ascribed to the Messiah in the book of Isaiah, meaning "God with us," which Hecht gives here in German.

It is twenty years now, Father. I have come home.
But in the camps, one can look through a huge square
Window, like an aquarium, upon a room
The size of my living room filled with human hair.
Others have shoes, or valises
Made mostly of cardboard, which once contained
Pills, fresh diapers. This is one of the places
Never explained.

Out of one trainload, about five hundred in all,
Twenty the next morning were hopelessly insane.
And some there be that have no memorial,
That are perished as though they had never been.[19]
Made into soap.
Who now remembers "The Singing Horses of Buchenwald"?[20]
"Above all, the saving of lives," whispered the Pope.[21]
Die Vögelein schweigen im Walde,[22]

But for years the screaming continued, night and day,
And the little children were suffered to come along, too.[23]
At night, Father, in the dark, when I pray,
I am there, I am there. I am pushed through
With the others to the strange room
Without windows; whitewashed walls, cement floor.
Millions, Father, millions have come to this pass,
Which a great church has voted to "deplore."

Are the vents in the ceiling, Father, to let the spirit depart?
We are crowded in here naked, female and male.
An old man is saying a prayer. And now we start
To panic, to claw at each other, to wail
As the rubber-edged door closes on chance and choice.
He is saying a prayer for all whom this room shall kill.
"I cried unto the Lord God with my voice,
And He has heard me out His holy hill."[24]

19. From Ecclesiasticus (also known as Sirach) 44:9 (a book included in Catholic and Eastern Orthodox Bibles but considered apocryphal in Jewish and Protestant traditions).

20. The Nazi SS forced prisoners to haul heavy carts while singing; they called them "singing horses."

21. According to *Jewish American Literature* (New York: W. W. Norton, 2001), ed. Chametzky et al.: "Alludes to the belief that Pope Pius XII—Eugenio Pacelli (1876–1958)—did not speak out enough against Nazi anti-Semitism."

22. According to Chametzky et al.: "'The little birds are silent' (German), from Goethe's *Wanderer's Night Song*, set to music by Schubert and others."

23. In the King James Version of Matthew 19:14, Jesus says, "Suffer [i.e., allow] little children, and forbid them not, to come unto me: for of such is the kingdom of heaven."

24. Psalm 3:4.

Denise Levertov
(1923–1997)

ADVENT 1966[25]

Because in Vietnam the vision of a Burning Babe
is multiplied, multiplied,
                                    the flesh on fire
not Christ's, as Southwell saw it, prefiguring
the Passion upon the Eve of Christmas,

but wholly human and repeated, repeated,
infant after infant, their names forgotten,
their sex unknown in the ashes,
set alight, flaming but not vanishing,
not vanishing as his vision but lingering,

cinders upon the earth or living on
moaning and stinking in hospitals three abed;

because of this my strong sight,
my clear caressive sight, my poet's sight I was given
that it might stir me to song,
is blurred.
                    There is a cataract filming over
my inner eyes. Or else a monstrous insect
has entered my head, and looks out
from my sockets with multiple vision,

seeing not the unique Holy Infant
burning sublimely, an imagination of redemption,
furnace in which souls are wrought into new life,
but, as off a beltline, more, more senseless figures aflame.

And this insect (who is not there—
it is my own eyes do my seeing, the insect
is not there, what I see is there)
will not permit me to look elsewhere,

or if I look, to see except dulled and unfocused
the delicate, firm, whole flesh of the still unburned.

---

25. *Advent*: The Christian season leading up to Christmas in anticipation of the birth of Christ.

Denise Levertov

from "Mass for the Day of St. Thomas Didymus"[26]

iii. Credo

I believe the earth
exists, and
in each minim mote
of its dust the holy
glow of thy candle.
Thou
unknown I know,
thou spirit,
giver,
lover of making, of the
wrought letter,
wrought flower,
iron, deed, dream.
Dust of the earth,
help thou my
unbelief. Drift,
gray become gold, in the beam of
vision. I believe and
interrupt my belief with
doubt. I doubt and
interrupt my doubt with belief. Be,
belovéd, threatened world.
            Each minim
mote.
            Not the poisonous
luminescence forced
out of its privacy,
the sacred lock of its cell
broken. No,
the ordinary glow
of common dust in ancient sunlight.
Be, that I may believe. Amen.

26. *St. Thomas Didymus*: The apostle, known popularly as Doubting Thomas, who touched Jesus' wounds after the resurrection (see John 20:24–29).

Yehuda Amichai
(1924–2000)

Near the Wall of a House

Near the wall of a house painted
to look like stone,
I saw visions of God.

A sleepless night that gives others a headache
gave me flowers
opening beautifully inside my brain.

And he who was lost like a dog
will be found like a human being
and brought back home again.

Love is not the last room: there are others
after it, the whole length of the corridor
that has no end.

Translated from the Hebrew by Chana Bloch and Stephen Mitchell

Relativity

There are toy ships with waves painted on them
and dresses with a print of ships at sea.
There's the effort of remembering and the effort of blossoming,
the ease of love and the ease of death.
A four-year-old dog corresponds to a man of thirty-five
and a one-day fly, at twilight, to a ripe old man
full of memories. Three hours of thought equal
two minutes of laughter.
In a game, a crying child gives away his hiding-place
but a silent child will be forgotten.
It's a long time since black stopped being the color of mourning:
a young girl defiantly squeezes herself
into a black bikini.

A painting of a volcano on the wall
makes the people in the room feel secure,
and a cemetery is soothing
because of all the dead.

Someone told me he's going down to Sinai because
he wants to be alone with his God:
I warned him.

Translated from the Hebrew by Chana Bloch and Stephen Mitchell

Zbigniew Herbert
(1924–1998)

BREVIARY

Lord,
    I know my days are numbered
    there are not many of them left
    enough for me to gather the sand
    with which they will cover my face

    I will not have enough time
    to render justice to the injured
    or ask forgiveness of all those
    who suffered evil at my hands
    that is why my soul is grieved

    my life
    should come full circle
    close like a well-built sonata
    but now I see clearly
    just before the coda
    the broken chords
    badly set colors and words
    the din of dissonance
    the tongues of chaos

    why
    was my life
    not like circles on the water
    welling from infinite depths
    like an origin which grows
    falls into layers rungs folds
    to expire serenely
    in your inscrutable lap

Translated from the Polish by Alissa Valles

Vassar Miller
(1924–1998)

COLOGNE CATHEDRAL

I came upon it stretched against the starlight,
a black lace
of stone. What need to enter and kneel down?
It said my prayers for me,

lifted in a sculptured moment of imploring
God in granite,
rock knees rooted in depths where all men
ferment their dreams in secret.

Teach marble prayers to us who know no longer
what to pray,
like this dumb worship's lovely gesture carven
from midnight's sweated dews.

DARK CYCLE

No prayer or penitence, no positive thinking,
No science, reason, neither spells of magic,
No courtroom pleadings clever, deftly tragic,
No devil-may-care tricks like boisterous drinking,
No methods professorial and pedagogic
Can stave it off a breath, elude by blinking

Away the black dog as Churchill used to call
His intimate darkness, Lincoln knew it too,
Did Shakespeare? Did Jesus? As ounce by ounce
The verse and praises throbbed? And maybe Paul
Besought God thrice against it—yet finally knew
God stopped the sun one time, but only once.

A. R. Ammons
(1926–2001)

HYMN

I know if I find you I will have to leave the earth
and go on out
        over the sea marshes and the brant[27] in bays
and over the hills of tall hickory
and over the crater lakes and canyons
and on up through the spheres of diminishing air
past the blackset noctilucent clouds
            where one wants to stop and look
way past all the light diffusions and bombardments
up farther than the loss of sight
        into the unseasonal undifferentiated empty stark

And I know if I find you I will have to stay with the earth
inspecting with thin tools and ground eyes
trusting the microvilli sporangia and simplest
        coelenterates
and praying for a nerve cell
with all the soul of my chemical reactions
and going right on down where the eye sees only traces

You are everywhere partial and entire
You are on the inside of everything and on the outside

I walk down the path down the hill where the sweetgum
has begun to ooze spring sap at the cut
and I see how the bark cracks and winds like no other bark
chasmal to my ant-soul running up and down
and if I find you I must go out deep into your
        far resolutions
and if I find you I must stay here with the separate leaves

---

27. *brant*: A kind of goose.

Luci Shaw
(b. 1928)

MARY'S SONG

Blue homespun and the bend of my breast
keep warm this small hot naked star
fallen to my arms. (Rest . . .
you who have had so far
to come.) Now nearness satisfied
the body of God sweetly. Quiet he lies
whose vigor hurled
a universe. He sleeps
whose eyelids have not closed before.

His breath (so slight it seems
no breath at all) once ruffled the dark deeps
to sprout a world.
Charmed by dove's voices, the whisper of straw,
he dreams,
hearing no music from his other spheres.
Breath, mouth, ears, eyes
he is curtailed
who overflowed all skies,
all years.
Older than eternity, now he
is new. Now native to earth as I am, nailed
to my poor planet, caught that I might be free,
blind in my womb to know my darkness ended,
brought to this birth
for me to be new-born,
and for him to see me mended
I must see him torn.

Geoffrey Hill
(b. 1932)

TENEBRAE[28]

He was so tired that he was scarcely able to
hear a note of the songs: he felt imprisoned
in a cold region where his brain was numb
and his spirit was isolated.

1

Requite this angel whose
flushed and thirsting face
stoops to the sacrifice
out of which it arose.
This is the lord Eros
of grief who pities
no one; it is
Lazarus with his sores.

2

And you, who with your soft but searching voice
drew me out of the sleep where I was lost,
who held me near your heart that I might rest
confiding in the darkness of your choice:
possessed by you I chose to have no choice,
fulfilled in you I sought no further quest.
You keep me, now, in dread that quenches trust,
in desolation where my sins rejoice.
As I am passionate so you with pain
turn my desire; as you seem passionless
so I recoil from all that I would gain,
wounding myself upon forgetfulness,
false ecstasies, which you in truth sustain
as you sustain each item of your cross.

---

28. *Tenebrae*: (Latin) "darkness"; the name of the Christian services observed in commemoration
of the death of Christ on the evening before or early morning of Maundy Thursday, Good Friday, and
Holy Saturday, the last three days of Holy Week.

3

Veni Redemptor, but not in our time.
Christus Resurgens, quite out of this world.
'Ave' we cry; the echoes are returned.
Amor Carnalis is our dwelling-place.[29]

4

O light of light, supreme delight;
grace on our lips to our disgrace.
Time roosts on all such golden wrists;
our leanness is our luxury.
Our love is what we love to have;
our faith is in our festivals.

5

Stupefying images of grief-in-dream,
succubae to my natural grief of heart,
cling to me, then; you who will not desert
your love nor lose him in some blank of time.
You come with all the licence of her name
to tell me you are mine. But you are not
and she is not. Can my own breath be hurt
by breathless shadows groaning in their game?
It can. The best societies of hell
acknowledge this, aroused by what they know:
consummate rage recaptured there in full
as faithfulness demands it, blow for blow,
and rectitude that mimics its own fall
reeling with sensual abstinence and woe.

6

This is the ash-pit of the lily-fire,
this is the questioning at the long tables,
this is true marriage of the self-in-self,
this is a raging solitude of desire,
this is the chorus of obscene consent,
this is a single voice of purest praise.

29. These Latin phrases should be understood in their ecclesiastical—and musical—contexts: *Veni Redemptor*: "Come, Redeemer"; *Christus Resurgens*: "Christ rising [from the dead]"; *Ave*: "Hail"; *Amor Carnalis*: "fleshly love."

Geoffrey Hill

7

He wounds with ecstasy. All
the wounds are his own.
He wears the martyr's crown.
He is the Lord of Misrule.
He is the Master of the Leaping Figures,
the motley factions.
Revelling in auguries
he is the Weeper of the Valedictions.

8

Music survives, composing her own sphere,
Angel of Tones, Medusa, Queen of the Air,
and when we would accost her with real cries
silver on silver thrills itself to ice.

Wendell Berry
(b. 1934)

To Know the Dark

To go in the dark with a light is to know the light.
To know the dark, go dark. Go without sight,
and find that the dark, too, blooms and sings,
and is traveled by dark feet and dark wings.

The Hidden Singer

The gods are less
for their love of praise.
Above and below them all
is a spirit that needs
nothing but its own
wholeness,
its health and ours.
It has made all things
by dividing itself.
It will be whole again.
To its joy we come
together—the seer
and the seen, the eater
and the eaten, the lover
and the loved.
In our joining it knows
itself. It is with us then,
not as the gods
whose names crest
in unearthly fire,
but as a little bird
hidden in the leaves
who sings quietly
and waits
and sings.

Leonard Cohen
(b. 1934)

IF IT BE YOUR WILL

If it be your will
that I speak no more,
and my voice be still
as it was before,
I will speak no more,
I shall abide until
I am spoken for,
if it be your will.

If it be your will
that a voice be true,
from this broken hill
I will sing to you.
From this broken hill
all your praises they shall ring
if it be your will
to let me sing.

If it be your will,
if there is a choice,
let the rivers fill,
let the hills rejoice.
Let your mercy spill
on all these burning hearts in hell,
if it be your will
to make us well.

And draw us near
and bind us tight,
all your children here
in their rags of light;
in our rags of light,
all dressed to kill;
and end this night,
if it be your will.

WHEN I LEFT THE KING

When I left the king I began to rehearse what I would say to the world: long rehearsals full of revisions, imaginary applause, humiliations, edicts of revenge. I grew swollen as I conspired with my ambition, I struggled, I expanded, and when the term was up, I gave birth to an ape. After some small inevitable misunderstanding, the ape turned on me. Limping, stumbling, I fled back to the swept courtyards of the king. "Where is your ape?" the king demanded. "Bring me your ape." The work is slow. The ape is old. He clowns behind his bars, imitating our hands in the dream. He winks at my official sense of urgency. What king? he wants to know. What courtyard? What highway?

I DRAW ASIDE THE CURTAIN

I draw aside the curtain. You mock us with the beauty of your world. My heart hates the trees, the wind moving the branches, the dead diamond machinery of the sky. I pace the corridor between my teeth and my bladder, angry, murderous, comforted by the smell of my sweat. I weakened myself in your name. In my own eyes I disgraced myself for trusting you, against all evidence, against the prevailing winds of horror, over the bully's laughter, the torturer's loyalty, the sweet questions of the sly. Find me here, you whom David found in hell. The skeletons are waiting for your famous mechanical salvation. Swim through the blood, father of mercy. Broadcast your light through the apple of pain, radiant one, sourceless, source of light. I wait for you, king of the dead, here in this garden where you placed me, beside the poisonous grass, miasmal homesteads, black Hebrew gibberish of pruned grapevines. I wait for you in the springtime of beatings and gross unnecessary death. Direct me out of this, O magnet of the falling cherry petals. Make a truce between my disgust and the impeccable landscape of fields and milky towns. Crush my swollen smallness, infiltrate my shame. Broken in the unemployment of my soul, I have driven a wedge into your world, fallen on both sides of it. Count me back to your mercy with the measures of a bitter song, and do not separate me from my tears.

Charles Wright
(b. 1935)

Georg Trakl Journal[30]

Sunday, first day of summer,
The whites of my eyes extinguished
                              in green and blue-green,
The white sleep of noon
Settling, a fine powder,
                    under the boxweed and overgrowth.
Windless, cloudless sky.
Odor of amethyst, odor of mother-of-pearl.
Beyond the mulched beds,
The roses lie open like a tear in the earth's side.
St. Thomas,[31] if he were here,
                    would put his hand just there.

Never forget where your help comes from.
Last year, and the year before,
                    the landscape spoke to me
Wherever I turned,
Chook-chook and interlude chook-chook and interlude
As I sat in the orchard,
Fricatives and labials, stops and chords
                    falling like sequins inside the shadows
The jack pines laid at my feet,
Little consonants, little vowels
For me to place on my tongue,
                    for me to utter and shine from.

Now silence. Now no forgiveness.
                    Not even a syllable
Strays through the fevered window
Or plops like a toad in the tall grass.
                    The afternoon
Dissolves in my mouth,
The landscape dwindles and whispers like rice through my dry fingers.

30. *Georg Trakl*: Austrian poet (1887–1914).

31. *St. Thomas*: The apostle, known popularly as Doubting Thomas, who touched Jesus' wounds after the resurrection. See John 20:24–29.

Now twilight. Now the bereft bodies
Of those who have never risen from the dead glide down
Through the dwarf orchard
And waver like candle flames
                       under the peach trees and go out.

Night, and the arbor vitae,[32] like nuns,
Bow in their solitude,
                 stars hang like tiny crosses
Above the ash trees,
Lamenting their nakedness.
                 Haloes of crystal thorns
Parachute out of the sky.
The moon, like a broken mouth,
Cloistered, in ruins, the vanished landscape,
Keep their vows, their dark patience.
Nothing says anything.
             Nothing says nothing.

32. *arbor vitae*: A kind of evergreen tree in the cypress family.

Alicia Suskin Ostriker
(b. 1937)

PRAYER IN AUTUMN

As to the deep ineradicable flaws
in the workmanship

anger and envy
anger and envy

stemming from overenthusiasm
that rises like a water lily from mud

and the stone
of self, of ego

that insists on its imperial monologue
that strangles its audience

I would like to repent but I cannot
I am ridden like a horse

What does the contriver have in mind
the contrivance wants to know

because otherwise what is the point
of all this moaning

pretending to be sorry for everything
groveling like a chained-up snake

crawling over a stone book
in the rain of words

for which someone is responsible
until at times the food devours the eater

the pot wishes to speak to the potter[33]
the clay chooses the hands

≈

We are not competent to make our vows
we are truly sorry

we pull you down from a cloud
or bend our knees to you like sideshow dogs

death breathing invisibly next to us on the bus
in the office in the kitchen on the park bench

we promise to love only you
faithful, faithful, we promise

we lie, we are not competent
still we implore you

please look at us and take us in your arms
not like a master, like a mother

33. See Romans 9:20&21: "But who are you, a human being, to talk back to God? Shall what is formed say to the one who formed it, 'Why did you make me like this?' Does not the potter have the right to make out of the same lump of clay some pottery for special purposes and some for common use?" (NIV).

Seamus Heaney
(b. 1939)

IN IOWA

In Iowa once, among the Mennonites
In a slathering blizzard, conveyed all afternoon
Through sleet-glit pelting hard against the windscreen
And a wiper's strong absolving slumps and flits,

I saw, abandoned in the open gap
Of a field where wilted corn stalks flagged the snow,
A mowing machine. Snow brimmed its iron seat,
Heaped each spoked wheel with a thick white brow,

And took the shine off oil in the black-toothed gears.
Verily I came forth from that wilderness
As one unbaptized who had known darkness
At the third hour and the veil in tatters.[34]

In Iowa once. In the slush and rush and hiss
Not of parted but as of rising waters.

34. These lines refer to the New Testament story of Jesus' crucifixion, during which there were three hours of darkness and the curtain in the temple that separated the Holy Place from the Holy of Holies was torn. See Matthew 27:45–53.

Robert Siegel
(b. 1939)

A.M.

Yellow flames flutter
about the feeder:
a Pentecost of finches.[35]

VOICE OF MANY WATERS

*To him that overcometh will I give to eat of the hidden manna, and
will give him a white stone, and in the stone a new name written,
which no man knoweth saving he that recieveth it.*[36]

The night is cluttered with stars.
    The drift of the earth
is dark, enormous
    bulking shoulder of the undersea whale
in the Atlantic's winking canyons.
    Trees wait
for the slow stain of day
    walking now over the water
west of England.

    I put two sticks on the fire
on the ghost of logs
    that fade into the red eye
drawing the circle of my campsite
    about which hang
my all-weather tent, glinting axe
    myself, like planets
inching the swarm of stars.

    Twelve o'clock:
The beast startles first with his foot
    broad as unbearable moon,
his leg the shank of stars

---

35. *Pentecost:* The biblical event when the Holy Spirit descended on Jesus' disciples, appearing as tongues of flame. See Acts 2.

36. Revelation 2:17 (KJV).

Robert Siegel

      his mane the black roar of space
turning to the white heart of fire
      in which begin to move
thick and uncertain

      the rivery shapes of trees
bending over water
      cradling a platinum light
running to gold
      and pebbles
each speckled with suns
      each turned and lapped by the water.

Green steals over me:
      I am swung in a net of leaves.
Birds wrap me tight in their songs:
      drunk with the trauma of flowers
I am and I hear a voice calling
      within the voices of water.
A shadow brightens the ground.
      A hand darkens all but itself.

Somewhere in the face of the trees
      a large clumsy beast is singing
the brood of pain and music
      played on the stops of the worlds
the flute of starlight and vacuum
      the unending theme of Abyss
and the trees are growing before me
      translating all to flowers.

Now the voice is within a white stone
      round in my hand like water
that speaks one word running through fingers
      to shred in my mouth like the moon.
Outside the sun is rising. Blue,
      the sky is blue
and the far forest neighing.

      I wake in the orange flower of my tent.

      for Clyde Kilby

Joseph Brodsky
(1940–1996)

DECEMBER 24, 1971

for V. S.

When it's Christmas we're all of us magi.
At the grocers' all slipping and pushing.
Where a tin of halvah, coffee-flavored,
is the cause of a human assault-wave
by a crowd heavy-laden with parcels:
each one his own king, his own camel.

Nylon bags, carrier bags, paper cones,
caps and neckties all twisted up sideways.
Reek of vodka and resin and cod,
orange mandarins, cinnamon, apples.
Floods of faces, no sign of a pathway
toward Bethlehem, shut off by blizzard.

And the bearers of moderate gifts
leap on buses and jam all the doorways,
disappear into courtyards that gape,
though they know that there's nothing inside there:
not a beast, not a crib, nor yet her,
round whose heads gleams a nimbus of gold.

Emptiness. But the mere thought of that
brings forth lights as if out of nowhere.
Herod reigns but the stronger he is,
the more sure, the more certain the wonder.
In the constancy of this relation
is the basic mechanics of Christmas.

That's why they celebrate everywhere,
for its coming push tables together.
No demand for a star for a while,
but a sort of good will touched with grace
can be seen in all men from afar,
and the shepherds have kindled their fires.

Joseph Brodsky

Snow is falling: not smoking but sounding
chimney pots on the roof, every face like a stain.
Herod drinks. Every wife hides her child.
He who comes is a mystery: features
are not known beforehand, men's hearts may
not be quick to distinguish the stranger.

But when drafts through the doorway disperse
the thick mist of the hours of darkness
and a shape in a shawl stands revealed,
both a newborn and Spirit that's Holy
in your self you discover; you stare
skyward, and it's right there:
                              a star.

Judy Little
(b. 1941)

ROSARY RECITATION

I.

A phrase flung, a beginning like a stone
Nudging a pool, the redundant circles muscling
Silent water and gathering a larger and larger
Center of lapsing ridges where the prayer-images
Float and stretch and breathe, like thin sunlight that swims
On its own reflection and rhythmically follows its new
Edges wave after wave and circle after silence,
The word-circles lifting the bright silence, rim
By rim, till the widening cup of light ripens,
Becomes shoreless, a world-large sea of breathing
And full as the tide when the moon-season pulls
And the waves labor to deliver the beginning all
Over again, and the lunging laughter from the ocean's
Heart brings to the home-shore surf after surf the deep world's
Joy, crest-breaking, thronging the laughter over and over.

II.

Beginning is a garden where birth sweats
And bleeds and prayer is no good anymore.
Touching the sand, the desert garden's green
Edges shrink. Now even the root will die.
The vineyard is abandoned. The earth breaks,
Cracked scarlet. The sand strikes. Sunlight descends
Too close for flesh. From breath to bursting breath,
From prayer to prayer, from morning to the evening,
The hard light lays waste the favored heart.
The throat, in such a thirsting light, crawls towards
Curses or psalms, and the voice, light-stricken, offers
The husk of itself to prayer-songs that time
Has ripened for despair, for absolute
Sorrow. The seed, sun-scarred, sacrifices its dust.

Judy Little

III.

Our words have disappeared into their sound.
Clear but buried syllables in the stream's voice
Glow, speechless as stones planted in the empty
Water. But who can speak of the other side
Of everything? Only the slant sunlight
Climbs the rainbow's crumbling rain. The oldest
Stars have lost themselves to find us. Their light,
Once we see it, is no longer there
But worn to illusion by the rapid trammels
Of unspoken space, the fossil star-prints tracking
The sky with empty spots of time, and endlessly
Shifting the red beginnings of their end,
And gathering beyond our sight into their dark
Unknown clouds of centering light, galactic
Wheels of homelight yet pouring itself to far
Spirals of trailing dance-tracks, the spilling light
By the heartful surging to time and planets that turn
From light to flesh, from flesh to light again,
Ascending and descending seeds, an arriving crown,
A glory that comes forever quickly, Amen, Amen.

Louise Glück
(b. 1943)

VESPERS

I don't wonder where you are anymore.
You're in the garden; you're where John is,
in the dirt, abstracted, holding his green trowel.
This is how he gardens: fifteen minutes of intense effort,
fifteen minutes of ecstatic contemplation. Sometimes
I work beside him, doing the shade chores,
weeding, thinning the lettuces; sometimes I watch
from the porch near the upper garden until twilight makes
lamps of the first lilies: all this time,
peace never leaves him. But it rushes through me,
not as sustenance the flower holds
but like bright light through the bare tree.

VESPERS

Even as you appeared to Moses, because
I need you, you appear to me, not
often, however. I live essentially
in darkness. You are perhaps training me to be
responsive to the slightest brightening. Or, like the poets,
are you stimulated by despair, does grief
move you to reveal your nature? This afternoon,
in the physical world to which you commonly
contribute your silence, I climbed
the small hill above the wild blueberries, metaphysically
descending, as on all my walks: did I go deep enough
for you to pity me, as you have sometimes pitied
others who suffer, favoring those
with theological gifts? As you anticipated,
I did not look up. So you came down to me:
at my feet, not the wax
leaves of the wild blueberry but your fiery self, a whole
pasture of fire, and beyond, the red sun neither falling nor rising—
I was not a child; I could take advantage of illusions.

Richard Jackson
(b. 1946)

TIDINGS

1. The Annunciation

Like a sentence you discover and read after too many
years, after you think the world's heart has turned
to dust, the air shriveling in your lungs, though
you cannot understand some of the words
for they seem like stars with no owners,
something like the ache of flowers for their seeds,
and you begin to realize it is a sentence
that celebrates what you could only imagine
like the canticles of mountain streams,
despite the black hearts perched, years later, on branches,
despite the moon thinning with hunger
then bloating like a starving child,
despite the tracer rounds streaming
like dandelion seeds the Child will blow across His room,
this sentence with its riverbed of stars,
this sentence that carries you too
the way a leaf is pulled downstream, because this,
you begin to realize, is not the song of a seed
fallen on stone, not some light scorched
into the dunes of the sky, but a phrase
whose wings fill the room, and you,—
you are that word which had remained
unnoticed in this sentence, and you begin
to speak with that light that quivers
like a branch, your own lips slightly moving
like a petal the bee has just left,
and you begin to realize you have lived
your whole life in this sentence
gradually unfolding towards its end,
the way the moon now plows the sky,
the way what you once thought was a mere star
now turns out to be a galaxy.

2. Three Kings

The sound was all yellow, the flower of the moon
opened. For a while we thought we were living
in the landscape of someone else's dream.
There was a fire that burned like an icicle from a rope.
Someone else said it might be a star.
He seemed to know something about the moon's scars,
so we followed. We tracked the ruts of the sky's song.
You can cut off the branches of a dogwood and still
see its outlines in the air. Sometimes our gaze
just crawled along the road carrying a burden
we somehow wanted. We knew how tight
the chains of our hearts held us.
When we went to the king you could hear the stars wilt.
We thought he wanted to tear the clouds from the sky.
The winds gathered in the mountains, plotting.
We could hear the cry of the trees, the desperate
snail clinging to a rock. Later we heard
the voice of mothers raging over the hills
like the glow of a fire. Everyone we met wanted
to blindfold the sky. It seemed there were clocks
inside their hearts. It seemed their eyes
were made of dust. When we finally arrived
it was as if we could see every blade of grass,
every seed's beginning, every cricket's song,
every star's desire. And then we could speak.
It seemed His words opened our own mouths.
Here was the universe in a husk of song.
Here was a city in a splinter of joy.
Here were our souls embracing like our smoky breaths.
Here was pure hope flowering in His eyes.

3. Joseph

And so the stars finally pelted us
with answers. Whatever tears we had were pressed
like olives. He came quietly then,
a stirring in the frost, a shuffling of the lamb's feet.
When the cold settled on his eyelids
it was as if a flock of doves lowered their quilt
down around us. It was then we knew that
the stars only wanted to drink from the pools
they seemed to live in, or become the insects
you could hear above the heartbeats of animals.
It was like lifting a stone to see another world,

a stone we had carried all that time.
Now the whole story will appear like the exposed roots
of a dogwood. Hope collects like dew in the desert night.
Even the hanged man will strangle his ropes.
It is our swords that will plow the sky.
Our lives are thumb prints in the air, which means
that soon all our dreams will wander on without us.
Our graves will fill their sails with light.
You can open their words like almonds.
You have to step into that river that flows inside you.
It is a world where suns are sown like seeds.
It is not easy, this beating your wings against the world.
Even now you can see the fingertips of His words
starting to knead the air into the shape of a prayer,
a sentence inscribed in your eyes that only you can read.

Stella Vinitchi Radulescu
(b. 1946)

SCREAM

I went too far, too far in the woods. The tree
was there, the body hanging
from a branch.

It was yesterday, I was looking for God.

Free from gravity, his legs in the wind
right, left . . .
a creepy balance between shadows and light.

Too far on Earth, too far into the night . . . I touched
the corpse, it went away in flames
and dust.

He is still here in the declining moon some words would fit
his skull

And I was scared, the scream
took my whole body with it, I thought I was flying . . .

But no, there I found myself stuck on the ground
from scream to scream building
an altar of silence.

STARTING POINT

1.
at the beginning of the light
the clock was set up to this very moment
a road was cut

life didn't happen for centuries
then my parents came and gave me flesh

here I am   a heart made out of frozen seconds
a second itself freezing in front of your eyes

Stella Vinitchi Radulescu

this is what makes this moment alive
my body to grow
to seek understanding

2.
and what if I fail and what if I don't
the day is not what you see the apple is not
what you want

desire keeps dripping around

this is how it is, the big lie which makes us feel
good
about our selves

forgive me for talking in no voice
for not bleeding peacefully like the sun

3.
the answer is in our hands
but we don't understand a long time ago

we named things at random
now we are paying for it

we don't see a soul like we see the moon rising
we don't understand simple facts

where are we going
why do the seagulls cry I have these words

sometimes I feel like touching their flesh
the roundness

and then I let them fall
one by one into your mouth, Mr. Nothing

make me an offer
I will buy your big and burning eyes

4.
now is the moment for the tide to rise for you to be here
to ask and to cry
to be young to be old   to check the weather
to bury your friend

now is the moment to make your bed
go to sleep

doucement doucement[37]
falling into a long dream

~

mirror of clouds
no earth no whispers
no hidden meaning under the shrine
nothing about snow
about us gripping the dark

we have learned the music

a second lit in our palms

37. *doucement*: (French) "softly" or "gently"—or, as an imperative, the equivalent of "Steady now."

Agha Shahid Ali
(1949–2001)

FROM "FROM AMHERST TO KASHMIR"

7. Film *Bhajan* Found on a 78 RPM

Dark god shine on me you're all I have left
nothing else blue god[38] you are all I have
I won't let go I'll cling on to your robe

I am yours your Radha[39] my bangles break
I break my bangles my heart is glass come back
blue god there's nothing you are all I have

let there be no legend of a lost one
who breaks her bangles who lets herself die
who says you hid yourself to break my heart

your eyes are my refuge hide me from the world
dark god Dark Krishna you are all I have
do not hide yourself merely to break my heart

all day I'm restless all night I can't sleep
the morning star sinks it drowns in my eyes
the night is heavy its dark is iron

take my hand place your hands in mine in yours
I'm yours dark god do not abandon me
all night I won't sleep even for a while

in the temples all the worshippers sleep
your flute strikes the stars its legends echo
and the soul in its trance crosses the sky

my heart keeps breaking does not stop breaking
it says dark god I will never leave you
the heart is awake it keeps on breaking

38. *dark god* and *blue god*: References to Krishna.
39. *Rhada*: Krishna's childhood friend and lover.

all night I'm awake I'll keep you awake
take this vow that I am yours I am yours
dark god you are all I have all I have

all night I'm awake I'll keep you awake
in your temples all the worshippers sleep
only swear I am yours that I am yours

only take this vow I am yours dark god
dark god you are all you are all I have
swear only swear I am yours I am yours

9. God

"In the Name of the Merciful" let night begin.
I must light lamps without her—at every shrine?
God then is only the final assassin.

The prayers end. Emptiness waits to take her in.
With laments found lost on my lips, I resign
myself to His every Name. Let night begin

without any light, for as they carry the coffin
from the mosque to the earth, no stars shine
to reveal Him as only the final assassin.

The mourners, at the dug earth's every margin,
fill emptiness with their hands. Their eyes meet mine
when with no Name of His I let my night begin.

In the dark the marble of each tomb grows skin.
I tear it off. I make a holocaust. I underline
God is the only, the only assassin

as flames put themselves out, at once, on her shrine
(they have arrived like moths from temples and mosques).
In no one's name but hers I let night begin.

Robert Cording
(b. 1949)

ADVENT STANZAS[40]

I.

Are we always creating you, as Rilke[41] said,
Trying, on our best days,
To make possible your coming-into-existence?

Or are you merely a story told in the dark,
A child's drawing of barn and star?

Each year you are born again. It is no remedy

For what we go on doing to each other,
For history's blind repetitions of hate and reprisal.

Here I am again, huddled in hope. For what
Do I wait?—I know you only as something missing,
And loved beyond reason.

As a word in my mouth I cannot embody.

II.

On the snow-dusted field this morning—an etching
Of mouse tracks declares the frenzy of its hunger.

The plodding dawn sun rises to another day's
One warm hour. I'm walking to the iced-in local pond

Where my neighbors have sat through the night
Waiting for something to find their jigged lure.

The sky is paste white. Each bush and tree keeps
Its cold counsel. I'm walking head-on into a wind

40. *Advent*: The Christian season leading up to Christmas in anticipation of the birth of Christ.

41. Rainer Maria Rilke (1875–1926) was a German poet—one of the greatest poets of the 20th century.

That forces my breath back into my mouth.
Like rags of black cloth, crows drape a dead oak.

When I pass under them, their cries rip a seam
In the morning. Last week a lifelong friend told me,

There's no such thing as happiness. It's ten years
Since he found his son, then a nineteen-year-old

Of extraordinary grace and goodness, curled up
In his dormitory room, unable to rise, to free

Himself of a division that made him manic and
Depressed, and still his son struggles from day to day,

The one partial remedy a dismal haze of drugs.
My friend hopes these days for very little—a stretch of

Hours, a string of a few days when nothing in his son's life
Goes terribly wrong. This is the season of sad stories:

The crippling accident, the layoffs at the factory,
The family without a car, without a house, without money

For presents. The sadder the human drama, the greater
Our hope, or so the television news makes it seem

With its soap-opera stories of tragedy followed up
With ones of good will—images of Santas' pots filling up

At the malls, truckloads of presents collected for the shelters,
Or the family posed with their special-needs child

In front of a fully equipped van given by the local dealership.
This is the season to keep the less fortunate in sight,

To believe that generosity will be generously repaid.
We've strung colored lights on our houses and trees,

And lit candles in the windows to hold back the dark.
For what do we hope?—That our candles will lead you

To our needs? That your gift of light will light
These darkest nights of the year? That our belief

In our own righteousness will be vindicated?
The prophet Amos knew the burden of your coming.

Robert Cording

The day of the Lord is darkness, he said, *darkness, not light,*
As if someone went into a house and rested a hand against a wall,

And was bitten by a snake. Amos knew the shame of
What we fail, over and over, to do, the always burning

Image of what might be. Saint Paul, too, saw
The whole creation groaning for redemption.

And will you *intercede with sighs too deep for words*[42]
Because you love us in our weakness, because

You love always, suddenly and completely, what is
In front of you, whether it is a lake or leper.

Because you come again and again to destroy the God
We keep making in our own image. Will we learn

To pray: May our hearts be broken open. Will we learn
To prepare a space in which you might come forth,

In which, like a bolt of winter solstice light,
You might enter the opening in the stones, lighting

Our dark tumulus[43] from beginning to end?

III.

All last night the tatter of sleet, ice descending,
Each tree sheathed in ice, and then, deeper
Into the night, the shattering cracks and fall
Of branches being pruned by gusts of wind.

It is the first morning after the longest night,
Dawn colorless, the sun still cloud-silvered.
Four crows break the early stillness, an apocalypse
Of raucous squawks. My miniature four horsemen

Take and eat whatever they can in the field
Outside my door: a deer's leg my dog has dragged
Home. Above them, the flinty sun has at last fired
A blue patch of sky, and suddenly each ice-transfigured
Tree shines. Each needle of pine, each branch
Of ash, throws off sparks of light. Once,

42. See Romans 8:26.
43. *tumulus*: Burial mound.

A rabbi saw a spark of goodness trapped inside
Each evil, the very source of life for that evil—

A contradiction not to be understood, but suffered,
The rabbi explained, though the one who prays
And studies Torah will be able to release that spark,
And evil, having lost its life-giving source, will cease.

When I finally open my door and walk out
Into the field, every inch of my skin seems touched
By light. So much light cannot be looked at:
My eyelids slam down like a blind.

All morning I drag limbs into a pile. By noon,
The trees and field have lost their shine. I douse
The pile of wood with gas, and set it aflame,
Watching sparks disappear in the sky.

IV.

This is the night we have given for your birth.

After the cherished hymns, the prayers, the story
Of the one who will become peacemaker,
Healer of the sick, the one who feeds
The hungry and raises the dead,

We light small candles and stand in the dark

Of the church, hoping for the peace
A child knows, hoping to forget career, mortgage,
Money, hoping even to turn quietly away

From the blind, reductive selves inside us.

We are a picture a child might draw
As we sing *Silent Night, Holy Night.*

Yet, while each of us tries to inhabit the moment
That is passing, you seem to live in-between
The words we fill with our longing.

The time has come
To admit I believe in the simple astonishment
Of a newborn.

And also to say plainly, as Pascal[44] knew, that you will live
In agony even to the end of the world,

Your will failing to be done on earth
As it is in heaven.

Come, o come Emmanuel,

I am a ghost waiting to be made flesh by love
I am too imperfect to bear.

---

44. Blaise Pascal (1623–1662) was a French mathematician, scientist, writer, and Catholic philoso-pher, famous for a collection of theological and philosophical writing known as *Pensées* (French for "thoughts").

Marie Howe
(b. 1950)

THE STAR MARKET

The people Jesus loved were shopping at The Star Market yesterday.
An old lead-colored man standing next to me at the checkout
breathed so heavily I had to step back a few steps.

Even after his bags were packed he still stood, breathing hard and
hawking into his hand. The feeble, the lame, I could hardly look at them:
shuffling through the aisles, they smelled of decay, as if The Star Market

had declared a day off for the able-bodied, and I had wandered in
with the rest of them: sour milk, bad meat:
looking for cereal and spring water.

Jesus must have been a saint, I said to myself, looking for my lost car
in the parking lot later, stumbling among the people who would have
been lowered into rooms by ropes,[45] who would have crept

out of caves or crawled from the corners of public baths on their hands
and knees begging for mercy.

If I touch only the hem of his garment, one woman thought, I will be healed.[46]
Could I bear the look on his face when he wheels around?

PRAYER

Every day I want to speak with you. And every day something more important
calls for my attention—the drugstore, the beauty products, the luggage

I need to buy for the trip.
Even now I can hardly sit here

among the falling piles of paper and clothing, the garbage trucks outside
already screeching and banging.

The mystics say you are as close as my own breath.
Why do I flee from you?

---

45. See Mark 2:1–5.
46. See Luke 8:43–48.

Marie Howe

My days and nights pour through me like complaints
and become a story I forgot to tell.

Help me. Even as I write these words I am planning
to rise from the chair as soon as I finish this sentence.

Suzanne Underwood Rhodes
(b. 1950)

SUNDAY SERVICE AT THE HOME FOR THE INCURABLES

Idiots
misfits
drooling fools
and spastics:

Forgive my sterile poise
and tidy clothes
and manners acquired
from much church
and so little rubbing
into your palsy and piss
and men asleep from birth
living in cribs.

Undo
me
dear
incurables singing
"My Jesus" in slapstick,
your hands with minds
of their own
shaking praise.

Moving in your midst
a tender light,
a love unkempt
and blind waits on you
singly, touching
each ragged grief, each

buried rage and sings
your circus hymns
with reverence,
as one who well knows
the pogroms of fools.

Touch me, my gargoyle
heart, and make
me
crow.

Suzanne Underwood Rhodes

The Gardener

I haven't talked to you about
a dark space I dug up.
Clods and rocks I can pick out of soil,
blue-veined clay I can nourish;
weeds, yank up; shade, cut back.
But this

hollow where no seed is meant to grow
astounds. I go back to basics,
trusting my hands to find the dirt
as it always was, humid and maternal,
easily worked to hatch seeds,
but this

breach of earth voids every breathing
speck so that the spade of my hand
weighs more than death, and the leaves
I touch are stillborn. Tell me,
must I keep tending, must I
turn this

blank into myself and vanish,
or is the hole an entrance
into some new ground that is yet
familiar, tilled and fertile, vast
as my loss, tenderly sown with
this?

Andrew Hudgins
(b. 1951)

PISS CHRIST

Andres Serrano, 1987[47]

If we did not know it was cow's blood and urine,
if we did not know that Serrano had for weeks
hoarded his urine in a plastic vat,
if we did not know the cross was gimcrack plastic,
we would assume it was too beautiful.
We would assume it was the resurrection,
glory, Christ transformed to light by light
because the blood and urine burn like a halo,
and light, as always, light makes it beautiful.

We are born between the urine and the feces,
Augustine says, and so was Christ, if there was a Christ,
skidding into this world as we do
on a tide of blood and urine. Blood, feces, urine—
what the fallen world is made of, and what we make.
He peed, ejaculated, shat, wept, bled—
bled under Pontius Pilate, and I assume
the mutilated god, the criminal,
humiliated god, voided himself
on the cross and the blood and urine smeared his legs
and he ascended bodily unto heaven,
and on the third day he rose into glory, which
is what we see here, the Piss Christ in glowing blood:
the whole irreducible point of the faith,
God thrown in human waste, submerged and shining.

We have grown used to beauty without horror.

We have grown used to useless beauty.

47. "Piss Christ" is one of Andres Serrano's controversial works of art, a photograph of a plastic crucifix submerged in the artist's urine.

Andrew Hudgins

Praying Drunk

Our Father who art in heaven, I am drunk.
Again. Red wine. For which I offer thanks.
I ought to start with praise, but praise
comes hard to me. I stutter. Did I tell you
about the woman whom I taught, in bed,
this prayer? It starts with praise; the simple form
keeps things in order. I hear from her sometimes.
Do you? And after love, when I was hungry,
I said, *Make me something to eat.* She yelled,
Poof! You're a casserole!—and laughed so hard
she fell out of the bed. Take care of her.

Next, confession—the dreary part. At night
deer drift from the dark woods and eat my garden.
They're like enormous rats on stilts except,
of course, they're beautiful. But why? What *makes*
them beautiful? I haven't shot one yet.
I might. When I was twelve, I'd ride my bike
out to the dump and shoot the rats. It's hard
to kill your rats, our Father. You have to use
a hollow point and hit them solidly.
A leg is not enough. The rat won't pause.
Yeep! Yeep! it screams, and scrabbles, three-legged, back
into the trash, and I would feel a little bad
to kill something that wants to live
more savagely than I do, even if
it's just a rat. My garden's vanishing.
Perhaps I'll merely plant more beans, though that
might mean more beautiful and hungry deer.
Who knows?
               I'm sorry for the times I've driven
home past a black, enormous, twilight ridge.
Crested with mist, it looked like a giant wave
about to break and sweep across the valley,
and in my loneliness and fear I've thought,
O let it come and wash the whole world clean.
Forgive me. This is my favorite sin: despair—
whose love I celebrate with wine and prayer.

Our Father, thank you for all the birds and trees,
that nature stuff. I'm grateful for good health,
food, air, some laughs, and all the other things
I'm grateful that I've never had to do
without. I have confused myself. I'm glad

there's not a rattrap large enough for deer.
While at the zoo last week, I sat and wept
when I saw one elephant insert his trunk
into another's ass, pull out a lump,
and whip it back and forth impatiently
to free the goodies hidden in the lump.
I could have let it mean most anything,
but I was stunned again at just how little
we ask for in our lives. *Don't look! Don't look!*
Two young nuns tried to herd their giggling
schoolkids away. *Line up*, they called. *Let's go
and watch the monkeys in the monkey house.*
I laughed, and got a dirty look. Dear Lord,
we lurch from metaphor to metaphor,
which is—let it be so—a form of praying.

I'm usually asleep by now—the time
for supplication. Requests. As if I'd stayed
up late and called the radio and asked
they play a sentimental song. Embarrassed.
I want a lot of money and a woman.
And, also, I want vanishing cream. You know—
a character like Popeye rubs it on
and disappears. Although you see right through him,
he's there. He chuckles, stumbles into things,
and smoke that's clearly visible escapes
from his invisible pipe. It makes me think,
sometimes, of you. What makes me think of me
is the poor jerk who wanders out on air
and then looks down. Below his feet, he sees
eternity, and suddenly his shoes
no longer work on nothingness, and down
he goes. As I fall past, remember me.

Mark Jarman
(b. 1952)

FROM *UNHOLY SONNETS*

Prologue

Please be the driver bearing down behind,
Or swerve in front and slow down to a crawl,
Or leave a space to lure me in, then pull
Ahead, cutting me off, and blast your horn.
Please climb the mountain with me, tailgating
And trying to overtake on straightaways.
Let nightfall make us both pick up the pace,
Trading positions with our high beams glaring.
And when we have exhausted sanity
And fuel, and smoked our engines, then, please stop,
Lurching onto the shoulder of the road,
And get out, raging, and walk up to me,
Giving me time to feel my stomach drop,
And see you face to face, and say, "My Lord!"

[Soften the blow, imagined God, and give]

Soften the blow, imagined God, and give
Me one good reason for this punishment.
Where does the pressure come from? Is it meant
To kill me in the end or help me live?
My thoughts about you are derivative.
Still, I believe a part of me is bent
To make your grace look like an accident
And keep my soul from being operative.
But if I'm to be bent back like the pole
A horseshoe clangs against and gives a kink to,
Then take me like the grinning iron monger
I saw once twist a bar that made him sink to
His knees. His tongue was like a hot pink coal
As he laughed and said he thought that he was stronger.

FIVE PSALMS

1.
Let us think of God as a lover
     Who never calls,
Whose pleasure in us is aroused
     In unrepeatable ways,
God as a body we cannot
     Separate from desire,
Saying to us, "Your love
     Is only physical."
Let us think of God as a bronze
     With green skin
Or a plane that draws the eye close
     To the texture of paint.
Let us think of God as life,
     A bacillus or virus,
As death, an igneous rock
     In a quartz garden.
Then, let us think of kissing
     God with the kisses
Of our mouths, of lying with God,
     As sea worms lie,
Snugly petrifying
     In their coral shirts.
Let us think of ourselves
     As part of God,
Neither alive nor dead,
     But like Alpha, Omega,
Glyphs and hieroglyphs,
     Numbers, data.

2.
First forgive the silence
     That answers prayer,
Then forgive the prayer
     That stains the silence.

Excuse the absence
     That feels like presence,
Then excuse the feeling
     That insists on presence.

Pardon the delay
     Of revelation,
Then ask pardon for revealing
     Your impatience.

Mark Jarman

Forgive God
     For being only a word,
Then ask God to forgive
     The betrayal of language.

3.
God of the Syllable
     God of the Word
God Who Speaks to Us
     God Who Is Dumb

The One God The Many
     God the Unnameable
God of the Human Face
     God of the Mask

God of the Gene Pool
     Microbe Mineral
God of the Sparrow's Fall
     God of the Spark

God of the Act of God
     Blameless Jealous
God of Surprises
     And Startling Joy

God Who Is Absent
     God Who Is Present
God Who Finds Us
     In Our Hiding Places

God Whom We Thank
     Whom We Forget to Thank
Father God Mother
     Inhuman Infant

Cosmic Chthonic[48]
     God of the Nucleus
Dead God Living God
     Alpha God Zed

God Whom We Name
     God Whom We Cannot Name
When We Open Our Mouths
     With the Name God Word God

---

48. *chthonic*: relating to the deity or deities of the Earth or the Underworld.

4.
The new day cancels dread
     And dawn forgives all sins,
All the judgments of insomnia,
     As if they were only dreams.

The ugly confrontation
     After midnight, with the mirror,
Turns white around the edges
     And burns away like frost.

Daylight undoes gravity
     And lightness responds to the light.
The new day lifts all weight,
     Like stepping off into space.

Where is that room you woke to,
     By clock-light, at 3 a.m.?
Nightmare's many mansions,
     Falling, have taken it with them.

The new day, the day's newness,
     And the wretchedness that, you thought,
Would never, never depart,
     Meet—and there is goodbye.

A bad night lies ahead
     And a new day beyond that—
A simple sequence, but hard
     To remember in the right order.

5.
Lord of dimensions and the dimensionless,
Wave and particle, all and none,

Who lets us measure the wounded atom,
Who lets us doubt all measurement,

When in this world we betray you
Let us be faithful in another.

Sofia M. Starnes
(b. 1952)

A WAY THROUGH WORDS

> *No utterance at all, no speech, not a sound to be heard . . .*
>   –Psalm 19

Now and in the hour:
after this, a temporary silence—come, let the air fall gently

on our laps, as if a fleece uncurling, nothing
else, as if a lamb we choose out of a herd, the sacramental.

After our histories of speech—harangues in song and stammer
with notices alighting on the trees—lean back: umber and

ancient on the chair, our trembling carriage.
Of hopes, this is the most unbearable yet true, our hardest moment.

After the tidying up of prayers, *Heart*, at the first,
Amen against the last exhaling, we're asked to finger quietness,

to flick the sediments of sound away, as one would sweep
a desert. Ah, dry against dry, the dust lured into puffs, the mouth

of nature: strong is the tongue that tastes.
Now and in the hour—

        One murmur—
And we've left this temporary silence, voices racing to tell us

what things are like. By rumoring, we raise the dead.
Blest be the word at stake, the universe of stars,

                          articulate as childbirth.

CLOSE TO THE TREE

> *I fell on the same ground that bears us all,*
> *and crying was the first sound I made.*
> –Book of Wisdom 7:3

I knelt and prayed for birth,
and so the sparrows brought
(as birds will often do)

ribs from a perfect nest.
      But then I specified,
anxious to make this true:

I need a body of bones,
a singularly pink heartbeat—
a cloudless voice.

      I prayed and asked
for words, something to mull
and chew, so ripe and succulent

my throat would grow its good,
eager . . .   Perched on its human
stem, it bore a hum as seed.

      And so the phrases came,
out of a simple root.
I was no longer wraith,

I was a futured girl, speaking—
of an eternity slim as a daylight
page (candle of eyelash wick, too

slender to be flare);
      of leaves that language
turns, of kisses made for hair,

bodies that hone a pulse
to keep their wrists at rest—
      restless, the holding place

      that holds this godly ache . . .

Richard Chess
(b. 1953)

DEAD LETTERS

> *cries like dead letters sent*
>   –Hopkins

Let the letters not be dead
as I am this morning, lifting the stone
book, opening prayer,
How goodly are thy tents, O Jacob.

Let the letters breathe, let them hum,
the ה (*hey*) and the מ (*mem*), let them declare
what's good, for I scarcely breathe, my pulse is feint.
Let your camp, Israel, vibrate.

How often have I turned to you, ע (*ayin*)
praying that the Nothing who gave you life
has not broken camp, withdrawn before I could proclaim,
How goodly are thy tents, O Jacob.

This morning when I saw my wife,
hair spilled on the pillow, open an eye,
and when our cold boy climbed in between us, I wanted
to sing, your camp, Israel, how good it is, alive.

But as if drugged or dead my tongue lay heavy.
Listening to radio in bed: while we slept, in Tel Aviv
another club on the beach, another blood-soaked crowd:
How goodly are thy tents, O Ya'akov?

Let the letters of the alphabet vibrate, let their voices
rage from my dumb hands, let their human prize
be delivered מה טבו אהליך יעקב (*mah tovu ohalekha Ya'akov*),
to dearest Him that lives, alas, away.

Jane Hirshfield
(b. 1953)

AGAINST CERTAINTY

There is something out in the dark that wants to correct us.
Each time I think "this," it answers "that."
Answers hard, in the heart-grammar's strictness.

If I then say "that," it too is taken away.

Between certainty and the real, an ancient enmity.
When the cat waits in the path-hedge,
no cell of her body is not waiting.
This is how she is able so completely to disappear.

I would like to enter the silence portion as she does.

To live amid the great vanishing as a cat must live,
one shadow fully at ease inside another.

Richard Jones
(b. 1953)

MIRACLES

I need to witness miracles today—
a river turned to blood,
water become wine,
a burning coal touching the prophet's lips,
black ravens swooping down
to bring a starving man bread and meat,
a poor fisherman raising the dead!
I've heard theologians say
this is not the age of miracles,
but still, I'm easy to impress.
I don't need to climb out of the boat
and walk on water; I'd just like
to put my head on the pillow
while the storm still rages, and rest.

Gjertrud Schnackenberg
(b. 1953)

SUPERNATURAL LOVE

My father at the dictionary-stand
Touches the page to fully understand
The lamplit answer, tilting in his hand

His slowly scanning magnifying lens,
A blurry, glistening circle he suspends
Above the word "Carnation." Then he bends

So near his eyes are magnified and blurred,
One finger on the miniature word,
As if he touched a single key and heard

A distant, plucked, infinitesimal string,
"The obligation due to every thing
That's smaller than the universe." I bring

My sewing needle close enough that I
Can watch my father through the needle's eye,
As through a lens ground for a butterfly

Who peers down flower-hallways toward a room
Shadowed and fathomed as this study's gloom
Where, as a scholar bends above a tomb

To read what's buried there, he bends to pore
Over the Latin blossom. I am four,
I spill my pins and needles on the floor

Trying to stitch "Beloved" X by X.
My dangerous, bright needle's point connects
Myself illiterate to this perfect text

I cannot read. My father puzzles why
It is my habit to identify
Carnations as "Christ's flowers," knowing I

Can give no explanation but "Because."
Word-roots blossom in speechless messages
The way the thread behind my sampler does

Gjertrud Schnackenberg

Where following each X I awkward move
My needle through the word whose root is love.
He reads, "A pink variety of Clove,

Carnatio, the Latin, meaning flesh."
As if the bud's essential oils brush
Christ's fragrance through the room, the iron-fresh

Odor carnations have floats up to me,
A drifted, secret, bitter ecstasy,
The stems squeak in my scissors, *Child, it's me,*

He turns the page to "Clove" and reads aloud:
"The clove, a spice, dried from a flower-bud."
Then twice, as if he hasn't understood,

He reads, "From French, for *clou*, meaning a nail."
He gazes, motionless. "Meaning a nail."
The incarnation blossoms, flesh and nail,

I twist my threads like stems into a knot
And smooth "Beloved," but my needle caught
Within the threads, *Thy blood so dearly bought,*

The needle strikes my finger to the bone.
I lift my hand, it is myself I've sewn,
The flesh laid bare, the threads of blood my own,

I lift my hand in startled agony
And call upon his name, "Daddy Daddy"—
My father's hand touches the injury

As lightly as he touched the page before,
Where incarnation bloomed from roots that bore
The flowers I called Christ's when I was four.

Franz Wright
(b. 1953)

THE ONLY ANIMAL

The only animal that commits suicide
went for a walk in the park,
basked on a hard bench
in the first star,
traveled to the edge of space
in an armchair
while company quietly
talked, and abruptly
returned,
the room empty.

The only animal that cries
that takes off its clothes
and reports to the mirror, the one
and only animal
that brushes its own teeth—

Somewhere

the only animal that smokes a cigarette,
that lies down and flies backward in time,
that rises and walks to a book
and looks up a word
heard the telephone ringing
in the darkness downstairs and decided
to answer no more.

And I understand,
too well: how many times
have I made the decision to dwell
from now on
in the hour of my death
(the space I took up here
scarlessly closing like water)
and said I'm never coming back,
and yet

Franz Wright

this morning
I stood once again
in this world, the garden
ark and vacant
tomb of what
I can't imagine,
between twin eternities,
some sort of wings,
more or less equidistantly
exiled from both,
hovering in the dreaming called
being awake, where
You gave me
in secret one thing
to perceive, the
tall blue starry
strangeness of being
here at all.

You gave us each in secret something to perceive.

Furless now, upright, My banished
and experimental
child

You said, though your own heart condemn you

I do not condemn you.

THE PROCESS

Unbidden it comes, without warning, and completely undeserved:
a mounting hallucinogenic
tranquility accompanied

by a slowing and, finally, total cessation of
time in which I freely and lucidly
move, make tea and so forth, muttering

words alone to myself, in a happiness
which for reasons best known to Yourself I was blessed with
from childhood on. And with alongside it

the long black killing years
of its infrequency or absence, that
can always come again,

according to Your will.
But when it does, this time
I will not whine, I will obey

and be
(forever)
still.

Scott Cairns
(b. 1954)

THE THEOLOGY OF DOUBT

I have come to believe this fickleness
of belief is unavoidable. As, for these
backlot trees, the annual loss
of leaves and fruit is unavoidable.
I remember hearing that soft-soap
about faith being given
only to the faithful—mean trick,
if you believe it. This afternoon,
during my walk, which
I have come to believe is good
for me, I noticed one of those
ridiculous leaves hanging
midway up an otherwise naked oak.
The wind did what it could
to bring it down, but the slow
learner continued dancing. Then again,
once, hoping for the last good apple,
I reached among bare branches,
pulling into my hand
an apple too soft for anything
and warm to the touch, fly-blown.

ADVENTURES IN NEW TESTAMENT GREEK: HAIRESIS

Surely ours would prove a far less tedious faith
all around if even a few among the more
zealous, more conspicuous brethren knew enough

to make a good heretic or two. My own glib
trespasses are clear enough, but when we're talking
heresy, I'd like to think I'm siding with the angels.

Hairesis finds its home in *choice*, in having chosen
one likely story over its more well received
counterpart, whose form—to the heretic—looks far

e, most heretics
n with something like
e *Good* as well

spoken quite as well
if any of us
te view.

would be the one
Vho by all
nut,

h slight,
orically—
t

im—, supposition
No,
he poor

reply with which the body has from time
to time addressed its more imaginative
members, but I would admit what shame

we share, allowing pettiness and fear
to acquire the faint patina of a virtue,
butchery, an ecclesiastical excuse.

Does one always *make* one's choices? From what
universal view of utter clarity
might one proceed? Let me know when you have it.

Even heretics love God, and burn
convinced that He will love them too.
Whatever choice, I think that they have failed

to err sufficiently to witness less
than appalling welcome when—just beyond
the sear of that ecstatic blush—they turn.

Scott Cairns

FROM "THE RECOVERED MIDRASHIM OF RABBI SAB"

3. The Sacrifice of Isaac

> *They arrived at the place*
> *of which God had told*
> *him. Abraham built an*
> *altar there; he laid out the*
> *wood; he bound his son*
> *Isaac; he laid him on the*
> *altar, on top of the wood.*
> *And Abraham picked up*
> *the knife to slay his son.*
> –Genesis 22:9&10

Who among us could bear the memory of Abraham's knife as it entered the heart of his son? Few enough, presumably. For why else has that incommensurate tableau been misrepeated so thoroughly?

In the stillness of that hour, the Lord pressed his servant inexplicably far and, despite the gentled features of a great many fables thereafter—the angel's intercession, the convenient goat, et cetera—, the knife found its cramping sheath there in the boy's bared breast, and blood covered both the boy and the father who embraced him even then, and blood colored the rock altar, rouged the mire underfoot.

In pity, then, the Lord briefly withheld time's aberrant fall, retracted the merest portion of its descent, sparked a subsequent visitation of the scene. This time, he stayed the hand, the knife, the rush of blood and of horror, but only in time.

Just outside time's arch embarrassment—in the spinning swoon of the I Am—the boy is bloodied still upon the rock, the man fallen upon him, left with nothing but his extreme, his absolute, his dire obedience.

Nicholas Samaras
(b. 1954)

THE UNPRONOUNCEABLE PSALM

I couldn't wrap my mouth around the vowel of Your name.
Your name, a cave of blue wind that burrows and delves
endlessly, that rings off the walls of my drumming, lilting heart,
through the tiny pulsations of my wrists, the blood in my neck.
I couldn't hold the energy of Your name in my mouth
that was like trying to utter the crackle of lightning,
as if my teeth would break from its pronunciation.
I am dwarfed in the face of Your magnitude,
O You whom I can't articulate. O You of fluency
and eloquence whom I can't fully express, my words
are only the echo of You that rings within my soul, my soul
a cave of blue wind that houses the draft of You,
the eternal vowel of You I can't wrap my mouth around.
Lord, Lord, as close as I may gather, as close as I may say.

PSALM AS FRUSTRATION I CAN LIVE WITH

I love the fierce wind outside my window
but know I would freeze in it.
I love the fierce wind from where I view it.
I love to wake and feel the presence of the Lord within.
I feel His presence only to lose it,
lose His presence only to feel it return.
I am seriousness which falls away from seriousness.
I control and lose control. I seize and lose grasp,
don't see and glimpse again.
I ration the irrational. I dive into ecstasy
and love the Lord as long as I can bear,
as I love the fierce wind outside my window.

Mary Karr
(b. 1955)

THE LAST OF THE BROODING MISERABLES

Lord, you maybe know me best
by my odd laments: My friend
drew the garage door tight,
lay flat on the cold cement, then
sucked off the family muffler
to stop the voices in his head.
And Logan stabbed in a fight, and Coleman shot,
and the bright girl who pulled a blade
the width of her own soft throat,
and Tom from the virus and Dad
from drink—Lord, these many-headed
hurts I mind.

        I study each death
hard that death not catch me
unprepared. For help I read Aurelius,
that Stoic emperor who composed
fine Meditations in his battle tent.

Surely he overheard at night
the surgeons chopping through
his wounded soldiers' bones
and shovels of earth flung down
on blue faces, and near dawn,
the barbarian horses athunder.

Still, he judged the young man's death
no worse than the old's: each losing
just one breath. I would have waded
the death pits wailing
till I ruined good boots with lime—
a vulture for my dead too long,
or half a corpse myself.

Lord, let me enter now
your world, my face,
dip deep in the gloves
of these hands formed
to sow or reap or stroke
a living face. Let me rise

to your unfamiliar light,
love, without which the dying
wouldn't bother me one whit.

Please, if you will, bless also
this thick head I finally bow. In thanks.

for James Laughlin

FOR A DYING TOMCAT WHO'S RELINQUISHED HIS FORMER HISSING AND PREDATORY NATURE

I remember the long orange carp you once scooped
        from the neighbor's pond, bounding beyond
        her swung broom, across summer lawns

to lay the fish on my stoop. Thanks
        for that. I'm not one to whom offerings
        often get made. You let me feel

how Christ might when I kneel,
        weeping in the dark
        over the usual maladies: love and its lack.

Only in tears do I speak
        directly to him and with such
        conviction. And only once you grew frail

did you finally slacken into me,
        dozing against my ribs like a child.
        You gave up the predatory flinch

that snapped the necks of so many
        birds and slow-moving rodents.
        Now your once powerful jaw

is malformed by black malignancies.
        It hurts to eat. So you surrender in the way
        I pray for: Lord, before my own death,

let me learn from this animal's deep release
        into my arms. Let me cease to fear
        the embrace that seeks to still me.

Patrick Donnelly
(b. 1956)

PRAYER OVER DUST

Into the kitchen bucket
go the bitter carrot tops,
collard ribs, burned heels,
drain-catcher leavings, useless
skins of things or their stringy hearts.

To these I've begun to add
my nail clippings and clumps
of hair that catch in the brush,
a way my mind chooses
to practice a hard thing.

But my body has lost interest
in the distinction between
Me and Not Me, rushes ahead
to the black box in the yard
with the mail-order worms:
fungus rings germinate
in my dark, moist places,
rash flashes up my torso,
my tongue wears white scum
and a sour, clabbered smell.

You, who cause the chemistry
of things coming apart
to give off an almost social warmth—
when it's over, let my body
be useful, let little bears
nose through my guts
for grubs, let Destroying Angel
lift its wild orchid umbrella
where my heart used to be.

Patrick Donnelly

On Being Called to Prayer While Cooking Dinner for Forty

When the heavens and the earth
are snapped away like a painted shade,
and every creature called to account,
please forgive me my head
full of chickpeas, garlic and parsley.
I am in love with the lemon
on the counter, and the warmth
of my brother's shoulder distracted me
when we stood to pray.
The imam takes us over
for the first prostration,
but I keep one ear cocked
for the cry of the kitchen timer,
thrilled to realize today's cornbread
might become tomorrow's stuffing.
This thrift may buy me ten warm minutes
in bed tomorrow, before the singer
climbs the minaret in the dark
to wake me again to the work
of thought, word, deed.
I have so little time to finish;
only I know how to turn the dish, so the first taste
makes my brother's eyes open wide—
forgive me, this pleasure
seems more urgent than the prayer—
too late to take refuge in You
from the inextricable mischief
of every thing You made,
eggs, milk, cinnamon, kisses, sleep.

Li-Young Lee
(b. 1957)

CHANGING PLACES IN THE FIRE

The wind in the trees
arrives all night at a word.

And the man who can't sleep
and the man who can't wake up
are the same man.

A memory of the ocean
torments the trees, a homesickness.

And the man who watches shadows of windblown leaves
and branches on the curtains,

the man who believes
a single page of the falling leaves restored
may be carried back to the living,

can't tell God's blind hand from God's seeing hand.

The wind, stranded in the branches,
like a memory of fire,

tells the oldest stories of Death
disguised as a traveler, or overlooked familiar,
friend we shunned for less
faithful playmates.

And the man who's afraid of the dark
and the man who loves the dark
are the same man.

A man who's afraid to die,
he would piece the tree back together,
each part numbered and labeled:
branch, leaf, breath, cry, glance.

A man who's afraid to live,
he thinks to himself: *Postpone all morning bells.*

The ore lies awake inside the rock, a dream
of origin pealing.

The bread that rises in a house that fails,
a man weeping.

The happy grain who elects the oven,
a man laughing.

And it isn't until the wind pauses
that he thinks he knows what it says.

It isn't until the man dismantles
wind, trees, listening, does he know
there is wind, there are trees, and no listening
but a dream of listening, a dream

with infinite moving parts,
hems, pleats, train cars, recurring stairs,
an imperfect past, a rumored present,
figures multiplied inside a mirror.

It isn't until he begins to wish
to sing
the whole flower
of his breathing, does he recognize
himself, a blossom mortally wounded on its stem.

Bruce Beasley
(b. 1958)

DAMAGED SELF-PORTRAIT

Then God said, 'Let us make man in our image, after our likeness.'
–Genesis 1:26

But tell me, who today has been able to record anything that comes across to us as a fact without causing deep injury to the image?
–Francis Bacon[49]

A shadow on the liver

—what the ultrasound
can't see,
clot of unmappable
flesh, dark mass

unimaged . . .

        So the occluded
self, the always-in-eclipse:
how to draw it

back, as the Infinite
shrank itself out of space, coiled down
to an infinitesimal
point, so that a universe, flawed,
not-God,
might have Its place.
The Kabbalists call it *zimzum*,
contraction, God
ridding the Creation of God,
self-

exilic, desacralizing
the cosmos even as He
gave birth to it—

---

49. Francis Bacon (1909–1992) was a British figurative painter (not to be confused with the Elizabethan philosopher of the same name).

Hence we remain ignorant of the true shape of the fireball—

—Hypernova
erupting in gamma-ray bursts
twelve-billion light years away,

for forty seconds more splendid than all
the rest of the universe
combined,
and no one can even tell

what it is,
what kind of "parent object"
could give birth to such a blast.

We can only measure
its afterglow in X-rays,
the satellite Beppo-Sax
tracing the untraceable
(*Ein-Sof*, the Kabbalists call God, No End, infinite, about Whom
nothing whatsoever may be said).

What's
known, what can
be said: Its host
galaxy at a redshift
of 3.42, correcting
for the flux calibration zero-point
and the galactic extinction . . .
Its measured

fluence
(the unknowable erupting out of itself)

and mine:
all the hoarded
silences, crystal
snowdrift
of the unsaid

(and the stubble that rises out of it).

If I could trace
such recesses
in me, so

Bruce Beasley

luminous, so obscure,
could I praise You again,
hosannah, as
a scab

clings to its cut?

Self-exilic, imaging
only the shadow, never the thing,
only the occultation
of these figures
of a self:
that crossing where the traffic light's
never green. Swamped
snag, the land
receding from it, at high tide; tide
always high. Glissandos, falling
scales, scales
falling from the eyes. Map-scales, and legends. Mapped

immensities—

          —*My likeness,*
There is something fierce and terrible in you,
eligible to burst forth

And no one can tell

what it is—

Hence we remain ignorant
of the true shape, the mirror's
helpless,
deformed mirroring.

          ∾

It's not the inside
of my body, not the shadow
of my liver at all,
not mine the five suspected
hemangiomas
the waves of the ultrasound
surround:

And so I draw
a self-portrait of withdrawal,

self-portrait as another's
concealed damage, my wife's
liver, shadowed, its textures

ambiguous, guessed-at . . .

       ∿

I want to make it like

but I don't know how to make it like:
Bacon, on trying to reproduce
in paint a sea-wave

says he can only make it like
obliquely (fragmented,
blurred, other
than what it seems): *Because appearances*
are ambiguous, this way of recording form
is nearer to the fact by its ambiguity of recording—

What artificial
likenesses—equations, damaged
figures:
(a cosmology with $H_0 = 65$ km s^{-1} Mpc^{-1})
Bacon's self-portraits in half-face, the loathed
features marred with globes of black, waves
of excrescence, seceding

from figuration.

       ∿

What Makes Mr. Bruce Beasley Tick:
personality portrait, compiled
by myself, on Mind Prober™ software
("A Complete X-ray of the Mind"):

a great many fears over day-to-day matters
keeps people at an emotional distance
may seem remote and silent
likely to act uninterested
avoids most situations others would enjoy
once in a long while you may notice he comes out of his shell

you are likely to see him turn away

Bruce Beasley

∾

In the beginning, Without End
took pleasure in Its own
autarkic self-sufficiency, there being

no other Being in the cosmos.
A shaking from Its isolation, as It coiled
deeper into Itself, having learned to need

an otherness, extra-
theos,
and so seceded

from what It made, imago Dei,[50] birth-
contractions,
contracting into Its own birth

(You are likely to see Him

turn away)

What Einstein wanted most to know: Did God ever have a choice?

∾

And now the eruptive, the self
made of all its X-ray traces,
host galaxies, redshifting
billions of light-years away:
Kierkegaard: The self is the conscious synthesis
of finitude and infinitude,
whose task is to become itself,
which can only be accomplished in relationship to God. Augustine:
But where was I
when I looked for You?
You were there before my eyes, but I had deserted
even my own self. I could not find myself,
much less find You. Eckhart: Outside of God,
there is nothing but nothing.

Dickinson: Me from Myself—to banish/Had I Art—
How this be
Except by Abdication—
Me—Of Me—

50. *imago Dei*: (Latin) "In the image of God." See Genesis 1:27.

≈

What Makes Mr. Bruce Beasley
Tick
(Mind Prober™ personality portrait,
compiled by my friends):

Wants intensely to be showered with attention
A natural performer, happiest when he has the spotlight
The ultimate experience for him is to be sought after by others
Although he tries to maintain his cool, his self-control gives way

Going it alone is not for him

≈

Autoluminosity, not-God

coming into being at the beginning of time
(nothing, but nothing)
gamma-rays' pilgrimage from then to now,
detected on December 14, 1997, at 5:34 p.m. CST
(an afterglow of 10^{53} erg, relativistic
ejecta)

Ejected
self, what the ultrasound can't see
(shadow, dark Mass unimaged)

celestial   "shocked gas"
            dimmed and reddened by dust

So dimmed,
dismembered
the metaphors of myself
(*zimzum*, gamma burst, mapped
immensities):

Shadow
of the hanging
scuppernong
where as a child I'd hide all day

Born
a twin, and as the moss
is ripped from a concrete wall,

Bruce Beasley

what green
particles still cling

Drawbridge,
jutting its halves over the river

Crucifix: awkward
overlay of two broken sticks

~

What kind of "parent object"
could give birth to such a blast:

Daddy in handcuffs, fire-
poker traced with blood

Mama's letters, script
palsied from vodka

Double-grave
by the crumbling mudbanks, kudzu's
creep across the dates

—*Always*
disrupting this literalness,
Bacon says,
because I find it quite easy and quite uninteresting

Eruptive,
        inward-
turning, against the literal,
the litter (lawn party,
little drinks with their umbrellas,
How is your summer going, are you taking any trips)
the shackled-
together letters of each word

(as the green
clings, the scab's
performed likeness to its cut)

Fuchsia drinks left over, with their umbrellas, in the rain

The shackled-together letters of the Word
a millisecond after the Big Bang

Self-portrait as something
other, the waves
of the ultrasound
pound against

ambiguity—

Emergence
from occultation (shadow,
injured
image, turning
away):

From distances and flux measurements
one can then infer

luminosities—

Marjorie Maddox
(b. 1959)

HER STATIONS OF THE CROSS[51]

I.
Here mothers move more than others
into Mary's mourning, each chorus
a soul full of crosses, weighted
with her child dying
continuously in the contemplation
of our contrition.

II.
That once-upon-a-time angel's voice
stretching anew her middle-aged womb,
she who once sang Magnify, O Magnify,
when all she screams for now
is mercy in her urgent rebirth
of sorrow.

III.
When he stumbles,
she cannot fix his fall,
cannot cradle the boyhood
scrapes and bruises bleeding
into crowd-sanctioned murder.
No cock crows; she hears his groans
as if the world's bones
are splintering within her.

IV.
Besides the tree, he carries
the tears of the one who carried him
beneath her Eve ribs, lifted him
into a world he breathed as good,
gone now into this God-crucified-
as-her-son catastrophe
for salvation's sake.

---

51. *Stations of the Cross*: A form of Catholic devotion organized around the 14 traditional events of
Christ's Passion—that is, the events leading up to and including his crucifixion and burial.

V.
Simon of Cyrene stands close.
Understanding too well the two sorrows—
mother and son helpless to comfort the other—
he heaves up and shoulders
the burdens of both,
his back the black tablet
of Moses' commandments fulfilled
to the jot and tittle.

VI.
Veronica—eyes swollen
for the Madonna and Child
wrenched from their rightful honor—
lifts her veil to cool the Savior's pain,
alleviate, however slightly, a mother's anguish.

VII.
Thorns gouge the brow she stroked.
The sweat-caked man that came out of her
stumbles again. Already,
the sharp nails gnaw her own palms.

VIII.
Oh, daughters of Jerusalem,
your tears sweep the streets,
wet the weary soles of Mary.
Weep for your own children
forever dashing away from Yahweh.[52]

IX.
Wretched stones that tip her sinless child,
dirt that drives down the innocent son.
His own earth hurts him more each tumble.
Three times he trips,
crashes to the dust we are,
mortal muscles turning their backs
on Man and his Mother.

X.
Threads twisted by her own fingers,
tugged carefully through cloth:
this is the tunic they rip from him,
fabric tattooed with red;
she remembers his baby body
blood-splattered and matted.

52. *Yahweh*: An anglicized version of the sacred name of God in the Hebrew scriptures.

Marjorie Maddox

XI.
Her soul stabbed by the tree
that slays her son. Her heart nailed.
She swears his life spurts
from her barely-breathing body.

XII.
Death is indigo and indelible,
the Roman sky collapsed and re-scribbled
on the shreds of her memories.
She cannot bear to look upon his face
when breath forgets its maker.

XIII.
Ten thousand stillborns better
than this: his torso in her arms,
icon of the inconsolable,
the flesh Pietà[53] with its nails of pain,
pounding, pounding.

XIV.
The hewn tomb seals her grief.
She remembers his first words,
his final prayer. All else rots
within her. They swaddle him,
implant him quickly behind stone.

---

53. *Pietà*: (Italian) "Pity"; a theme in Christian art in which Mary the mother of Christ is depicted holding Christ's body after the crucifixion.

Eric Pankey
(b. 1959)

Homage

1.
O my God, looming and rough-hewn,
Forge me with rage. If this is the purge
Ferret out and scald the cold grub
Burrowed in at my heart. Let havoc
Consume its nest and larder.
Let your gold cauter stanch the wound.

2.
Fall inviolate sledge, and be known.
Blast away the sawdust and matchwood,
The ash-fall and rusted filings.
Let me be your wedge, let that edge
Gleam from use, burnished as it divides
The flawed from this hammerdressed[54] world.

---

54. *hammerdressed*: Roughly shaped with a stonecutter's hammer.

Carl Phillips
(b. 1959)

HYMN

Less the shadow
than you a stag, sudden, through it.
Less the stag breaking cover than

the antlers, with which
crowned.
Less the antlers as trees leafless,

to either side of the stag's head, than—
between them—the vision that must
mean, surely, rescue.

Less the rescue.
More, always, the ache
toward it.

When I think of death, the gleam of
the world darkening, dark, gathering me
now in, it is lately

as one more of many other nights
figured with the inevitably
black car, again the stranger's

strange room entered not for prayer
but for striking
prayer's attitude, the body

kneeling, bending, until it finds
the muscled patterns that
predictably, given strain and

release, flesh assumes.
When I think of desire,
it is in the same way that I do

God: as parable, any steep
and blue water, things that are always
there, they only wait

to be sounded.
And I a stone that, a little bit, perhaps
should ask pardon.

My fears—when I have fears—
are of how long I shall be, falling,
and in my at last resting how

indistinguishable, inasmuch as they
are countless, sire,
all the unglittering other dropped stones.

Harry Newman
(b. 1961)

CRYSTAL LAKE

Averrill Park, NY

can this be the first time
I've seen geese arcing
above me straining
the sky with their calls

or the first I've woken
to a woodpecker's
insistent rapping from
the trees in the morning

or had deer so close
as they pad through
grass towards the water

have I grown this old
and the world so foreign
still I've only a child's
knowledge to guide me

pictures of the animals
I'd touch on the page
believing they were real
cartoon drawings with

the names given to me
deer woodpecker goose
an Adam in reverse and

all I have for this long trip
from Eden outlines colors
and the surfaces of things

Malaika King Albrecht
(b. 1965)

ON THE SHORE AT HOLDEN BEACH

I.

High tide reveals
in every beginning
an end.

The sea asks, *How strong*
will you stand? Rises and falls
all around you.

No matter where
we die, we're buried
at sea.

Once my daughter nearly drowned,
blue lips and
the sound of waves
inside her chest.
      Cut adrift,
we clung to a hospital bed
for three days until she
thrashed ashore—
said *I want to go home.*

II.

She finds a whole
sand dollar in the surf,
places it in my palm. *Don't*
lose it, mommy. Squeeze tight.

I say *No, it will break.*

How to teach her
that a fist
is how life catches us
in the jar of our own desire
to hold, to count

what we think is ours.
I show her, *Hold your hands*
with the sand dollar
between your palms.

Like we're praying, she says
walking gently back to shore.

SOUND KNOWS ITS PLACE IN THE AIR

> *You don't have a soul. You are a soul. You have a body.*
> —C. S. Lewis

I.

Seeing becomes a study
of loss in slow motion.
A single grain of sand falls
and another and another.
A handful of sand—
not a beach and yet
all I can hold.

II.

There are no longer angels
in the flames. We have left
the fires untended on the beach,
and some have gone out.
I cannot invent
the exact light
of Your name.

IIII.

We are inconsequential
to the dance, but music
fills the air around us,
ocean waves, heart beats.
Grace lifts itself from the hems
of our tongues,
and we listen with
our whole bodies.
I will not say your name
though I believe
it was You who called me.

Maurice Manning
(b. 1966)

FROM BUCOLICS

I

boss of the grassy green
boss of the silver puddle
how happy is my lot
to tend the green to catch
the water when it rains
to do the doing Boss
the way the sun wakes up
the leaves they yawn a bit
each day a little more
for a tiny reason then
when the leaves outgrow their green
the wind unwinds them Boss
that's the way you go around
if you loose me like a leaf
if you unburden me
if I untaste the taste
of being bossed by you
don't boss me down to dust
may I become a flower
when my blossom Boss is full
boss a bee to my blue lips
that one drop of my bloom
would softly drop into
your sweetness once again
if I go round that way
I'll know the doing means
to you what it means to me
a word before all words

XII

why Boss why do the days drift by
like a leaf asleep on a bed of water
does the leaf forgive the tree that let
it fall into the water does
it know how stiff the river's face

can be how smileless rivers like
to be at least this one Boss not a flinch
or bristle bloomed on its glassy face
the moment the leaf lay down no joy
no breathy gasp from the river's lips
when all the leaf was trying to do
is cuddle Boss does cuddling move
the likes of you are you the river or
the thing that makes the river's face
so still if a thing so little as
a leaf decided to cuddle up
to me I couldn't stand it Boss
I couldn't stare it down like you
I'd have to say you hush now leaf
you hush your little mouth good night

XIV

if you had a feed sack Boss what
would you keep inside a rooster or
a snake do you need to carry things
around I wonder if you hold
a rooster by his feet a snake
behind its head just think a snake
can't carry anything is that
a shame or is it all right Boss
the way things are is just the way
things are it's neither good nor bad
is that what I'm supposed to think
it doesn't matter if you have
a feed sack Boss not one whit to me
you can carry what you want the way
I carry on I wear myself
to pieces but that's just what I mean
O everything gets carried Boss
even if it never moves
I wonder if you ever notice
but sometimes Boss I carry you

LXXII

you leave a little night inside
the flower Boss to keep it closed
although the sun is up above
the middle branches of the tree
the flower has a little night
inside it I can see it Boss
a drop of pitch a pinch of sleep
as if the flower wants the night
to last a little longer than
it does I'm like the flower Boss
sometimes I want the night to last
so I can keep on sleeping when
I'm sleeping I don't have to think
about you Boss it's harder than
a summer field that hasn't seen
the rain for days to think about
you Boss do you know that you stone
you're hard to get around you're like
the morning always there when my
eyes flutter open when they see
the daylight coming softly that's
a laugh a thing so hard it starts
out easy Boss when I wake up
I feel a feather on my face

Christian Wiman
(b. 1966)

EVERY RIVEN THING

God goes, belonging to every riven thing he's made
sing his being simply by being
the thing it is:
stone and tree and sky,
man who sees and sings and wonders why

God goes. Belonging, to every riven thing he's made,
means a storm of peace.
Think of the atoms inside the stone.
Think of the man who sits alone
trying to will himself into a stillness where

God goes belonging. To every riven thing he's made
there is given one shade
shaped exactly to the thing itself:
under the tree a darker tree;
under the man the only man to see

God goes belonging to every riven thing. He's made
the things that bring him near,
made the mind that makes him go.
A part of what man knows,
apart from what man knows,

God goes belonging to every riven thing he's made.

ONE TIME

1. Canyon de Chelly, Arizona

Then I looked down into the lovely cut
of a missing river, something under
dusk's upflooding shadows
claiming for itself a clarity
of which my eyes were not yet capable:
fissures could be footpaths, ancient homes

random erosions; pictographs, depicting fealties
of who knows what hearts, to who knows what gods.
To believe is to believe you have been torn
from the abyss, yet stand waveringly on its rim.
I come back to the world. I come back
to the world and would speak of it plainly,
with only so much artifice as words
themselves require, only so much distance
as my own eyes impose
on the slickrock whorls of the real
canyon, the yucca's stricken
clench, and, on the other side,
the dozen buzzards swirled and buoyed
above some terrible intangible fire
that must scald the very heart
of matter to cast up such avid ash.

2. 2047 Grace Street

But the world is more often refuge
than evidence, comfort and covert
for the flinching will, rather than the sharp
particulate instants through which God's being burns
into ours. I say God and mean more
than the bright abyss that opens in that word.
I say world and mean less
than the abstract oblivion of atoms
out of which every intact thing emerges,
into which every intact thing finally goes.
I do not know how to come closer to God
except by standing where a world is ending
for one man. It is still dark,
and for an hour I have listened
to the breathing of the woman I love beyond
my ability to love. Praise to the pain
scalding us toward each other, the grief
beyond which, please God, she will live
and thrive. And praise to the light that is not
yet, the dawn in which one bird believes,
crying not as if there had been no night
but as if there were no night in which it had not been.

C. Dale Young
(b. 1969)

NATURE

Half-joking, half-serious, seriously halved,
I wanted to find Him in the empty sleeve
of air surrounding the bell's clapper.

Would He not be found there, hovering
in the air prepared to carry sound? So many
silly ideas the adolescent carries around.

So many of us vowed chastity, the easy gesture
for those who had denied their own nature.
But Nature could not be ignored—the way it

snaps the heads off mice, takes the hatchlings
one by one, breaks the mule's back. I understood
the rules. We all did. Rule #1: show kindness

to your brother. I wanted to show more
than kindness, wanted to favor my brothers,
for lack of a better word. Rule #2: do unto others . . .

I won't even go there. What point in that now?
There was always God reclining in the empty space
beside my hand, beside the thenar eminence,[55]

beside my careful eyes that imagined the other
boys in all of their happiness. In every man, God
had placed Himself. In every man, I sought

to touch that God. Silly, I know. Silly.
What I wanted then was to break God's heart—
I wanted Him to snap my neck, break my back.

55. *thenar eminence*: An anatomical term for the fleshy area of the palm at the base of the thumb.

SEPSIS

The fog has yet to lift, God, and still the bustle
of buses and garbage trucks. God, I have coveted
sleep. I have wished to find an empty bed

in the hospital while on call. I have placed
my bodily needs first, left nurses to do
what I should have done. And so, the antibiotics

sat on the counter. They sat on the counter
under incandescent lights. No needle was placed
in the woman's arm. No IV was started. It sat there

on the counter waiting. I have coveted sleep, God,
and the toxins I studied in Bacteriology took hold
of Your servant. When the blood flowered

beneath her skin, I shocked her, placed the paddles
on her chest, her dying body convulsing each time.
The antibiotics sat on the counter, and shame

colored my face, the blood pooling in my cheeks
like heat. And outside, the stars continued falling
into place. And the owl kept talking without listening.

And the wind kept sweeping the streets clean.
And the heart in my chest stayed silent.
How could I have known that I would never forget,

that early some mornings, in the waking time,
the fog still filling the avenues, that the image
of her body clothed in sweat would find me?

I have disobeyed my Oath. I have caused harm.
I have failed the preacher from the Baptist Church.
Dear God, how does a sinner outlast the sin?

Morri Creech
(b. 1970)

DOGWOOD

So this is what remains
of Christ in winter,
after the wounded petals
have dried and scattered
and the blown red leaves blaze
earthward. My father
told me its trunk once bore
the savior's body,
and for years I believed
the shadow of the one
outside my window
passed over me in judgment.

All season it brooded
over my mother's flowerbed,
her cabbage roses and hydrangeas,
long after she left my father.
And though he pulled
the slick maze of their roots
from the ground
next spring, he let the tree
abide there in the shade
of its own flourishing,
knelt and labored in silence
as the branches swelled
with patience and light.

Rooted half in soil, half in rumor,
warped tree of the garden,
for years the cleft in its trunk
has divided the twin boughs
of my belief and doubt.
Every night that winter
my prayers ascended its crown
and found no answer,
just as I imagine my father
prayed for strength or love.

Every night its bare limbs
scraped against the house
and blackbirds settled
in the heaven of its branches.

PROVISION

Nothing we tried could coax sweetness
from my grandfather's apple tree.
Year after year we tended the branches,
propped the broken boughs with scraps of lumber.
Year after year those hunched limbs
dragged the ground and bore a withered fruit
nothing could eat, not even the neighbor's horses.
So who cared when, one winter, lightning
tore a smoldering seam down its trunk?
My grandfather left the tree alone all season,
figuring the rain-soaked husk not fit for burning.

That April, axes in hand, we crossed the field
to clear the warped remains. My grandfather
leaned down and stuck his hand inside
the storm-struck hollow, as though
to touch the blighted heartwood.
He jerked his hand back, cursing, wringing fire
from his palm—and as we ran toward the house
the whole tree seemed to come alive at once,
swarming and quickening with bees
that had settled there to make honey in the wound.

Philip Metres
(b. 1970)

VOTIVE IVORY ON DISPLAY: NICODEMUS BELOW THE CROSS[56]

Because the dead grow so heavy, as if
    wanting the earth
below them, and because we cannot stand
    the sight of them,

their gravity, we leave the gravesite even
    before the hole
is filled with dirt. You refuse to leave
    your dead father.

From the silence of our car, we look at you,
    sobbing, no sounds
reach us. Your face wild with rage. Your arms hold
    your own body

growing heavy, your fingers rub beneath
    your eyes, as if
to wear away what lay before us. In the votive,
    it's so easy

to mistake Nicodemus for the crucifier,
    his hammer poised
over Christ's ivory wrists, his face wild
    with fear. His hand

will strike the nail away, hold the body until
    blood runs its course,
then lay it down. In the votive, the last flecks
    of olive, dun, and red

—the artist's paints—river the veins
    of the deepest cuts
only. No thorns of gold, no gem-encrusted
    cross, no tesserae-

---

56. *Nicodemus*: A Pharisee and member of the Sanhedrin (the Jewish ruling council at the time of Christ) who assisted in the burial of Christ. See John 3, 7:50&51, and 19:39.

shattered image of a god. Just a body
     cradling a body
carved in elephant's tusk, small enough
     to carry. An ancestry

of hands worrying, worrying the ivory
     features smooth.

from "A Book of Hours"

1.

You threw me down, Lord, on the bed
I did not know I was making, unmade,
Your arms held me down, Lord, and I could feel
The panic of stasis, could taste the bitter

Of ends, the tunnel of unbreathing,
Lord, you pressed your terrible weight
Against the whole length of my indivisible
Body, your invisible inexorable weight,

Your hands around my neck until I could see
Nothing but the black in front of me,
Your hurting whole behind me, in me now

Shivering, praying for this prison of skin
To release this voice to air, that these needle nerves
Unshackle the this I am, the this you are.

2.

Lord, I am not worthy, I am unweal-
Thy without you, but I am not unwilled,
Am not still in you. Yes, my soul is rest-
Less and does not rest in you, my Lord,

And I'm not ready to be seized by you
In receiving you. Unsteady in swells
Of you, I'm unmasted in the squall of you
In the sea of you, cannot outlast you.

Philip Metres

But only say the word and I shall be
Hurled from all hurt, thrown beyond shoals, unswal-
Lowed in shallows. Say the word and I shall

Be held, will the world and I shall be born,
Say it and I shall be beheld and hold
You, my Lord, say it with my mouth, I'm yours.

Jennifer Grotz
(b. 1971)

DOUBT

In the image of utter doubt, Thomas's accusing finger
probes into the wound of Christ.[57]
Nature returns silence but nature does not

say no, that's what humans do.
The rest of creation glorifies God: "The birds
sing to him, the thunder speaks of his terror . . .,

the honey is like his sweetness . . . . They give him glory
but do not know they do . . .
But man can know God, can mean

to give him glory. This was why he was made" [58] and this is why
we are cursed with self–consciousness, why Herbert[59] wrote,
"I read and sigh and wish I were a tree."

In the material world, things that are invisible
but exist are either too tiny or too far away.
Which, God, are you? Even doubt can

be concrete. On a cold morning
I have seen how the sun can only melt
the frost shadow doesn't cling to, how

shadow itself, rimed with ice, gleams.
In the image of utter faith,
Abraham holds a knife above the throat of his son Isaac,
ready to slice. Faith or doubt, which is more obscene?

Vulnerable, labial, violated, Christ too looking down at it,
the pierced wound penetrated
                            by Thomas's finger,
and the skin of his forehead bunched like a dress hiked up
to reveal the lewdness of those gaping eyes.
And what does it mean to him now that the wound is real?

57. See John 20:24–29.

58. This is a quote from Gerard Manley Hopkins (1844–1889), priest and poet.

59. *Herbert*: George Herbert (1593–1633), priest and poet.

Jennifer Grotz

SNOWFLAKES

Yesterday they were denticulate as dandelion greens, they
locked together in spokes and fell so weightlessly

I thought of best friends holding hands.
And then of mating hawks that soar into the air to link their claws
and somersault down, separating just before they touch the ground.

Sometimes the snowflakes glitter, it's more like tinkling
than snow, it never strikes, and I want to be struck, that is

I want to know what to do. I begin enthusiastically,
I go in a hurry, I fall pell–mell down a hill, like a ball of yarn's

unraveling trajectory—down and away but also in surprising ricochets
that only after seem foretold. Yesterday I took a walk because

I wanted to be struck, and what happened was
an accident: a downy clump floated precisely in my eye.

The lashes clutched it close, melting it against the eye's hot surface.
And like the woman talking to herself in an empty church

eventually realizes she is praying, I walked home with eyes that melted snow.

Philip Memmer
(b. 1971)

PSALM

Searching for you is like staring
    at the late afternoon's
    low sun: almost

I can tell myself I see you,
    until I realize
    that I face you

with both eyes shut, and the dazzle
    I might have called truth is
    my own bright blood.

PARABLE

Crammed through the eye of the needle,
    the camel ambled off
    to paradise,

knowing of his close scrape nothing
    but the actual walk,
    discomfiting

for sure, but less so than the whips
    he left behind, the long
    trails, the trials

of the wind-blown sands. Unclouded
    by metaphysics, deaf
    to the shouting

of his masters, he spat on the
    hallowed ground, then tramped on,
    forgivably

ungrateful. And you who would learn:
    you are not the camel.
    Nor are you one

of the servants—it took seven—
  who shoved him through that gate.
  What then is left?

You are the gate. And though today
  you remain untarnished,
  through you a world

must pass, stinking and braying. It
  will not thank you. It will
  pay you in flies.

Sufjan Stevens
(b. 1975)

CASIMIR PULASKI DAY[60]

Goldenrod and the 4-H stone—
the things I brought you when I found out
you had cancer of the bone.

Your father cried on the telephone
and he drove his car into the Navy yard
just to prove that he was sorry.

In the morning, through the window shade,
when the light pressed up against your shoulderblade
I could see what you were reading.

Oh, the glory that the Lord has made,
and the complications you could do without
when I kissed you on the mouth.

Tuesday night at the Bible study
we lift our hands and pray over your body,
but nothing ever happens.

I remember, at Michael's house,
in the living room, when you kissed my neck
and I almost touched your blouse.

In the morning, at the top of the stairs,
when your father found out what we did that night
and you told me you were scared.

Oh, the glory when you ran outside
with your shirt tucked in and your shoes untied
and you told me not to follow you.

Sunday night when I clean the house
I find the card where you wrote it out
with the pictures of your mother.

---

60. *Casimir Pulaski Day*: A public holiday in Illinois celebrating a Polish-born cavalry officer who fought in the American Revolution—the holiday referred to in line 35.

Sufjan Stevens

On the floor at the great divide,
with my shirt tucked in and my shoes untied,
I am crying in the bathroom.

In the morning when you finally go,
and the nurse runs in with her head hung low,
and the cardinal hits the window—

in the morning, in the winter shade,
on the first of March, on the holiday,
I thought I saw you breathing.

Oh, the glory that the Lord has made,
and the complications when I see His face
in the morning in the window.

Oh, the glory when He took our place,
but He took my shoulders and He shook my face,
and He takes and He takes and He takes.

Daniel Westover
(b. 1975)

OF FLESH AND HEAVEN

I admit it beckons me, that storied place
of harps and hymns and haloed seraphim.
I confess I lift eyes skyward; that I raise
my hands toward the stars, and that I dream
of wings. But the comforts of familiar earth:
a midnight binge; the sweet, soft grind of sex;
dry-biting gin, and velvet haze of sloth
pull me, are Sirens singing from the rocks.

This is, of course, my station: stuck between
chimp and cherub; lord of animals,
yet heaven's leper. Even as the sun
inspires me to shin up these mortal walls,
I cover my eyes, squint in its brilliance,
crawl back to my penumbral comfort zone,
where certainties of flesh quick-blunt the sense
of wanting to discard my blood and bone.

Don't get me wrong, though. I'm not saying no
to all the trumpets, thrones, and ivory towers.
I'd love a long silk robe, a gilt halo,
a white-washed mansion with a splash of flowers.
But might I, sometimes, lie in bed for days
and watch slow shadows inch across the walls?
Or is that heaven, like the good book says,
devoid of darkness, downtime, idle lulls?

I can't deny celestial towns tempt me—
imagination paves their roads with gold
as you'd expect: all burnished, blemish-free—
but I wonder: when we've overcome this world,
will perfect wings grow heavy on our backs?
How long before, like Icarus, I glide
toward the sun, so that the fastening wax
will melt, and send me crashing back to shade?

Daniel Westover

FROM "A PRAYER'S LOST LANGUAGE"

6. Stone River

Vitosha Mountain, outside Sofia

I have stood here before
on boulders large as cottages,
leapt over each wedged crevasse
that slants darkly down
and leads to buried water.

Downstream, a woman
leads her son across the clefts.
She jumps first, then turns
to pull small hands
over each gap of shadow.
The child's fear turns to laughter
with each safe landing.

A stork flaps from a far tree
and drags its ragged wingshade on the rocks.
The child sees it, and the woman
removes a woven broach from his coat;
he takes it, leans, still holding her hand,
and drops it between two stones.

I've learned this ritual—the *mártenik*
worn red or white at winter's end,
then cast away for luck and health
when spring's first stork
is seen above the trees.
Last March, on the pier in Varna,
when I saw a brown stork
tilt its wings above the waves,
I unpinned a red-stitched heart
from my once-white collar
and tossed it in the Black Sea.

Today I have no broach to throw;
no prayer forms on my lips;
but water feels its way below the rocks,
and the words I've spoken to God
still pull at me.

I came here two years ago
and thought myself called—
an elect zealot, quick
to give God's grace to godless communists.
I am still here. I have not turned
on my father's faith,
have not called back
a single prayer I've spoken,
but there are voices in this land
more fathomless than mine.

These hands, once set
to fall on the faithless,
to quicken tight tongues
with the spirit's wind,
have turned over
to show their empty palms.

The mother moves on; the boy
jumps faster now, his black boots
scuffing tops of stones.
Their voices weaken as the gap
grows slowly wider between us
until all I hear
as I sit above the river
is the quiet voice of stones.

Jericho Brown
(b. 1976)

THE BURNING BUSH

Lizard's shade turned torch, what thorns I bore
Nomadic shepherds clipped. Still,
I've stood, a soldier listening for the word,
Attack, a prophet praying any ember be spoken
Through me in this desert full of fugitives.
Now, I have a voice. Entered, I am lit.
Remember me for this sprouting fire,
For the lash of flaming tongues that lick
But do not swallow my leaves, my flimsy
Branches. No ash behind, I burn to bloom.
I am not consumed. I am not consumed.

Michael Schiavo
(b. 1976)

OF SONG[61]

believe
time

    filled
    high

heaven
is

life
shows

    I
    write

        fresh
        numbers

    to
    say

such
touches

    should
    with

        like
        truth

    true
    be

of
song

    some
    time

        you
        live

61. According to the author, these are "dub versions of Shakespeare's sonnets," in which he has chosen two words per line per sonnet, then arranged those words, in the order in which they originally appear, into couplets.

Michael Schiavo

RIOT THERE

        pretty
        liberty

            I
            thy

        beauty
        well

for
art

        gentle
        art

            beauteous
            art

        &
        a

will
till

        thou
        my

            &
            beauty

        riot
        there

art
break

        beauty
        thee

            by
            beauty

TIRED ALL

tired
all

    as
    born

&
nothing

&
faith

    &
    gilded

        &
        virtue
    &
    perfection

&
sway

    &
    art

        &
        skill

    &
    simple

&
good

    tired
    all

        to
        love

Ilya Kaminsky
(b. 1977)

AUTHOR'S PRAYER

If I speak for the dead, I must leave
this animal of my body,

I must write the same poem over and over,
for an empty page is the white flag of their surrender.

If I speak for them, I must walk on the edge
of myself, I must live as a blind man

who runs through rooms without
touching the furniture.

Yes, I live. I can cross the streets asking "What year is it?"
I can dance in my sleep and laugh

in front of the mirror.
Even sleep is a prayer, Lord,

I will praise your madness, and
in a language not mine, speak

of music that wakes us, music
in which we move. For whatever I say

is a kind of petition, and the darkest
days must I praise.

ENVOI

> *You will die on a boat from Yalta to Odessa.*
> –a fortune teller, 1992

What ties me to this earth? In Massachusetts,
the birds force themselves into my lines—
the sea repeats itself, repeats, repeats.

Ilya Kaminsky

I bless the boat from Yalta to Odessa
and bless each passenger, his bones, his genitals,
bless the sky inside his body,
the sky my medicine, the sky my country.

I bless the continent of gulls, the argument of their order.
The wind, my master
insists on the joy of poplars, swallows,—

bless one woman's brows, her lips
and their salt, bless the roundness
of her shoulder. Her face, a lantern
by which I live my life.

You can find us, Lord, she is a woman dancing with her eyes closed
and I am a man arguing with this woman
among nightstands and tables and chairs.

Lord, give us what you have already given.

Amit Majmudar
(b. 1979)

FROM *AZAZIL*

> *He [Azazil] was told: Bow down! He said, "I will bow to no other." He*
> *was asked, Even if you receive My curse? He said, "It does not matter. I*
> *have no way to an other-than-You. I am an abject lover . . . . There can*
> *be no distance for me. Nearness and distance are one . . . . A servant of*
> *pure heart will bow to no other than You."*
>
> –Mansur Al-Hallaj, The TaSin of Before-Time and
Ambiguity[62]

In the beginning, I was a word in His mouth. I slept under His soft, wet tongue. I came out wet, like a human baby, but I was smokeless fire, and I burned His saliva caul away. When the magma slowed and the earth cooled down and mist rose white off the black stopped magma, He pointed and said, *That was what you looked like. Only what's black there was blaze.*

I remember He took me riding in the whirlwind once. I was the only angel invited inside it. Its cockpit was a noiseless sphere, see-through. We went around inspecting the underbellies of black holes for signs of light. He said, *Here, Azazil, you can steer.*

I had my arms crossed over my chest. My knees touched my elbows. I was scared to touch the walls circling me.

Be Me, Azazil, and will it left.

The whirlwind banked. I was, like all the angels back then, Him.

But I was different than the other angels, though I did not know it yet. Closer.

Jibril asked me, eyeing my wind-mad hair, "What does that mean, 'Be Me'? We can't be Him. To say we and He are the same . . . that's blasphemous."

The others nodded to either side of him. He was their leader. And that was only right. He was, after all, one of them.

"We don't will *as* Him, Azazil. He wills *for* us. We must have misheard."

These were distinctions. I did not understand distinctions, in those days. I wasn't far enough away to see Him whole and look down and see me whole and think, those are two different things. Unlike Jibril, I really believed what we recited.

Say: Allah is One . . . .

---

62. Al-Hallaj, Mansur. "Iblis as Tragic Lover (The TaSin of Before-Time and Ambiguity)." In *Early Islamic Mysticism: Sufi, Qur'an, Mi'raj, Poetic and Theological Writings*, edited and translated by Michael A. Sells, 272–280. The Classics of Western Spirituality. New York, Mahwah: Paulist Press, 1996.

They saw us as bricks of the same mosque. I saw us as drops of the same wine, and not in the glass, either, but on His tongue, eternally being tasted.

We called our prayer the Unity. They said the Unity to Him, and they said it in unison.

All those voices, saying it at the same time: all wrong.

I said the Unity alone. When I said it, one voice said it.

His.

"He can't possibly have said *Be Me*, Azazil. That wouldn't make any sense. The whirlwind's so loud, it's not your fault. He must have said something else. Like . . . *Obey Me*."

I did not know I was different yet. But He knew.

I was the third living thing He made after light and water. He had not yet decided how far away He wanted angels to stand. So I turned out less . . . less *differentiated* than the others.

What I mean is, they were servants, I was a limb.

That is why He entrusted me with dawn.

The Greeks tell a story about Sisyphus. He rolls a heavy stone up a hill, and he gets to the top, and it rolls down the other side, and he has to start over. He's being punished like that.

I did the same thing, but for me it was an honor. I pushed the sun out of the east sea all the way to noon, then let it roll on its own weight into the west. When I got to noon and the sphere started rolling away from me, I would clap my hands with joy and chase it barefoot down the mosque dome sky.

You cannot handle a star from dawn to noon and not get burned. Even if your hands are made of smokeless fire, you can't.

Allah said to me, *The scar tissue webbing your palms is as beautiful to me as your face.*

I was a part of Him. When He cut me off with an ax called Adam, He bled, and I bled. He cried, and I cried.

A servant could have been sent away and called back. I was a limb, and there was no reattaching me.

How can someone be All-Powerful and incomplete at the same time?

I imagine Him turning Adam this way and that, pressing different sides of man to the stump where I used to be.

The Catastrophe happened aeons in. He decided water and light were not life enough for earth.

He wanted the dirt it was made of to live, too.

Amit Majmudar

We were fashioned out of His voice. We came out smokeless fire because that is what thought is, and He alone can say thought raw.

Adam He fashioned out of His blood. He mixed His blood with hard dirt, and the dirt slucked and softened under the heels of His hands.

A new emotion, the first other than ishq[63] I had ever felt, interrupted my love like a hiccough.

It wasn't envy, not at first. It was disgust.

Not even Jibril was comfortable with things. The planets were matter slums, dumps for elements too clunky to disperse or burn. Earth in particular. It wasn't like some planets, the gaseous ones, that made their own light. Earth was cosmos clutter.

And there Allah was—kneeling in it, forearms flecked with it.

"These species You are making," Jibril worried, "they are going to shed each other's blood someday. And the blood they shed will be Your own."

Allah said nothing, busy kneading flesh.

I said nothing. I trusted him, back then.

He brought me there and showed me by moonlight.

I call this species Man.

"Have you named him yet?"

No.

"What are you going to name him?"

I want you to name him, Azazil.

I climbed into His lap and thought about it.

"Adam."

I like that name. Adam he is.

"Adam."

Go closer to him. I brought you here so you get to be the first, Azazil.

"The first to touch him?"

Not yet—he's still cooling.

"The first to do what, then?"

Bow to him.

Denying Him exhilarated me in a way bliss didn't.

I had known the word "no" till then only from prayers affirming His Oneness. The same word made us two now.

How odd it felt to use that word in isolation! I took the Unity apart and found blasphemy in one of its components. *No.*

I was His limb—paralyzed at His side.

We were obedience and ishq, only more ishq. Adam? All obedience. Only through grace, verse, or drugs could that creature ever work himself up into ishq. Ishq even then a feeling, momentary. Not a state.

63. In Islam, *ishq* is a self-effacing love for Allah.

152

"Obedience to this command," pronounced Jibril, "is the only way we can stay in favor."

This was before the War. We argued in earshot of the perplexed angels.

"We have to acknowledge two masters now, Azazil."

"That's sacrilege," I declared. I got a few nods.

"Not in this case." Jibril was always the academician. "Really it's only one master: When we bow to Allah's khalif, we are really bowing to Allah, albeit through a thin pane of glass."

"It's not a window, it's a wall. Not glass, either. Mud. And why erect something between Him and us in the first place?"

It was easy for the others. Jibril, too, already *had* someone between him and Allah.

Adam and me or just me, the distance was infinite or twice infinite. But I was flush. Interposing Adam required severing Azazil.

"If we don't bow, we'll be exiles in our own bodies."

"Do you really believe He values obedience over ishq?"

"Of course!"

Jibril sounded surprised; so did I: "How can you *think* such a thing, Jibril?"

"I'm not . . . . He's thinking it for me."

Allah projected, on the bare white walls of their minds, bulletins, calming images, orders of the day.

Obey Me.

There is no God but Me.

Everything depends on Me.

I stared at my mind and saw my own desires streaked there in childish crayon, the receptive purity defaced.

He's thinking it for me.

That is one definition of blessedness: being thought for.

Which would make damnation having to think for yourself. To steer, to generate, to choose. To pour perceptions into a mind with a hole in its memory. To *will*.

If willing is suffering, who wills all? Who was first in the universe ever to will? Who was damned before Azazil?

I joined Him.

How we warred:

Two black bees in a bobbing sunflower.

In the North, the aurora borealis.

On the plains, brushfires; ignis fatuus[64] over water.

64. *ignis fatuus*: Phosphorescent light seen at night over marshy ground, caused by spontaneous combustion of gas generated by decomposing organic matter.

Swallows, mated for life, pecking a hawk back into the clouds. *Leave our young alone.*

Underwater, in chariots drawn by teams of leviathans.

As scorpions in a ring, tails high, circling.

Hemorrhage of ishq and ichor.[65]

Wind passing wind, catching; abruptly torqued. We drilled into the ground as one tornado.

In a sky crosshatched with threads of flash.

Biceps and triceps that pulled at the same elbow.

Panting, wings flaccid, against facing asteroids.

Allahu akbar their warcry, our warcry *Allahu akbar.*[66] Allah listened in and corrected neither side.

Dog barking at dog across a light year.

A bruise, spreading its blue faith.

In the South, migrations; massacres in the East.

Two stags locked and skidding dustily down a raw-rock mountainside.

Octopi, knotted. Leeches mouth to mouth, sealed.

Azazil–Jibril.

Eventually he intervened. He had to; I was winning.

I kept a staff of angels to track all the comets in the universe. They broadcast the warning to my forces in the field: new comets, over twenty of them.

Bright boils swelled on the skin of space and ruptured into speed. Hatched, the comets flew in a V for earth.

Except one. The largest broke off and steered for the asteroid where I had pinned Jibril.

The comets were not sentient fire, as we angels were. They were drones.

Did He love them, too?

When I was hit, Jibril was choking words of pity past my thumbs on his throat.

"He says you're infected. And you're infecting the others. He can heal you."

"Infected?" I did not ease up. And yet—*infection*—something outside me, acting on me—it would explain everything. "Infected with what?"

"*Will.*"

I was light years toward hell when I came to. My spine draped like a streamer over the nose of the comet.

I turned in a fitful coma before I finally awoke. So my face burned, too.

The scar tissue webbing your palms, He once told me, *is as beautiful to me as your face.*

I wonder if that is still true.

65. *ichor*: In Greek mythology, the fluid that flows in the veins of gods.

66. *Allahu akbar*: (Arabic) "Allah is the greatest."

Worst burned were my wings and back. They healed as one ridged mound. I went from winged dawn to hunchback.

I had my fellow exiles chip ice scalpels off a lake. It took three days' surgery to free my wingbone fans. Ashen rubber clung between their storm-snapped umbrella prongs.

I was as landbound as Adam.

Blinded soldiers wandered the snow. Some begged me to cut the weights from their ankles. There were no weights, of course, no ball and chain. Just gravity.

We were not used to gravity. The ground was covered with its sticky, invisible web. We were caught in it. It pulled at every arm and leg, spiderspit.

I wasn't born knowing how to fly. No bird is.

He held me over his head, hands around my waist, and said, *Move your wings up and down. Good.*

Held me like a father teaching his son to swim, the son shivering and scared but trusting him as he's carried from the pool wall.

He walked me out over an abyss, still holding me.

I kept moving my wings.

He let go, and I stayed where He had held me. I was not sure whether my wings suspended me or His proud gaze.

What do you mean you won't bow? Are you too proud to bow where your Lord tells you?

Seeing was not much different than not seeing, the darkness was so thick. If you stuck your arm out your hand disappeared. It was like dunking a torch underwater.

You could be standing in a crowd and never know it. That was how He wanted things. Unity was heaven's principle, atomization, hell's.

We had joined against Him. Now, to punish us, He kept us apart—from each other, and from Him.

For the first weeks no one said anything.

No stirring addresses out of me, no great monologues, no exhortations. The last thing devastation does is speechify. That would be action.

Despair, at its purest, shuts the body down. That's why people don't commit suicide until the upswing. Suicidal is the floor above hell.

We survived by tonguing Qu'rans into the snow, that we might read the text if a sun should rise someday.

We survived in contemplation. In regret.

By burning ourselves anew to sculpt our own scar tissue. By base jumping in the hope our wings might snag the air.

We clawed holes in the snow to find ground. When we found ground, we clawed farther, but our world's core had gone cold.

In cartography. In deriving a whole astronomy from the starlessness over our heads.

We splashed the shallow puddles that melted at our feet. Lift one foot and it flash froze around the other ankle.

Ishq I had in abundance. On ishq we survived. We survived on a ration of five prayers and a thousand tears a day.

I had seen Adam up close. I had seen the hairs that grew out of him—a whole body colonized with black grass. The skin wrinkled at his knuckles, the fingers' flesh sleeves too long, bunching when they straightened. When he turned in his sleep, the dirt kept a print in his shape.

This was the ugliest thing about him, to an angel. His solidity. How he blocked light instead of intensifying it. How the ground recorded him, and the air swirled in and out of him. He was a bone stuck in the throat of dissolution.

[. . .]

I never said I will not bow. I said I *cannot* bow.

He wouldn't ask Adam to violate a law of physics, would He? Yet He asked me to violate a law of metaphysics, and raged when I couldn't. Acted like it was my choice not to bow in two directions, when it's the equivalent of standing in two places at the same time.

[. . .]

Steven C. Brown Jr.
(b. 1980)

JULY'S ENTOMOLOGY

July's insect sun, its hive above the yard
drips white blinding sugar on our tongues.
The kids are strung along the leaves, cocoons
of so little memory but what is shared
by the maple's limb, that red festoon
of birds, those frogs of *sturm und drang*[67]—

becoming what the senses always urged,
what they always meant by *being*. This span
of trees, loose follicles of leaf, the star
of synapse where sight and knowledge merge
into one upheaval of the dead's desire:

What could it possibly mean other than
the magi's return to light-imbibing fields
where grows the germ and mystery of faith?

And if not Christ, then the hive's collective arm—
something giant that finds us in its world,
not as strangers, but as daughters of the worm,
a tongue unwhorled from the butterfly's mouth.

LATE HOURS FOR THE HARVESTERS

Even now, in the braid of cornstalk,
the shred of wind against the field, it's there—

the earth calls back the callipered ribs of harvesters.
The bright heads and husk go dark as root beneath the hill,
dark as the eye of killdeer closed.

There's a knowing in the closed mouths of wheat.
The migrant birds talk of winter coming on
and dig around the Osage root for scrap and hulls.

---

67. *sturm und drang*: (German) "Storm and stress." 1. The name of a late 18th century German literary movement. 2. Turmoil.

Steven C. Brown Jr.

The combine scrapes the field with bright teeth,
sheds the cropgold,
lays bare the dirt's cold ribs—

I cannot tell you what I mean.
The sky is closed against the locust earth.
Its vagrant apparition heads west toward the Pacific.

Hurricanes stalk the Gulf,
and grackles claw the cane field,
ripping at the cambium and bitterroot,
but they do not stop at the root.

They pick each stalk to the screaming crib of night.
And the moon, a lemur's small, sharp tooth,
cuts the field with a false light,

and the farmers, enclosed by the caw of dark birds,
keep their talk to the swinging scythe
and their heads low.

Their needle threads what's left of human need
to the root and seed of an earth
they cannot hear, that cannot talk
but through the rib of dirt we share.

The earth's bright palm is closed—
I cannot tell you what I mean.

There, in the field, there's a knowing—
something in our bones has failed,
which echoes far below the mantle's crust.

The heads of black cattle scour the barren ground,
clothed in parasitic dust.
They gnaw the promiseroot
while sowers, dressed in thin ribs,
keep on sowing
in the late night's rattled talk.

There's a knowing here in the Godroot beds,
in the work of sharp metal and mouths closed;
its language calls lightning to the field.

Tarfia Faizullah
(b. 1980)

ACOLYTE

The white cross pales
further still,
        nailed arms
watchful as window-light

furls over backs of our knees,
lavender shadows
        cutting across
our young necks

in this makeshift classroom
church. I kneel with
        the others, restless
on the cracked leather

kneeler—I crave these
white pillars of candle,
        while my hungry
tongue sings

fidelis, fidelis.[68]
I imagine Mother
        in her kitchen
humming black

and white Bollywood songs. She
curls her hennaed fingers
        around the rolling pin's
heavy back and forth

while Father rocks
in his chair, the Qur'an
        on his desk open to the last
page, the dark words

68. *fidelis*: Possibly a reference to the original Latin version of the Christmas hymn "O Come All Ye Faithful."

Tarfia Faizullah

blurring as his eyes close,
see again the shapla-flower
            shaped epitaph
on my sister's tombstone.

With my head bowed,
I whisper *amar naam*
            Tarfia[69] until it is
a prayer that grows.

I help stack the hymnals
higher, then
cup the candlelight away.

RAMADAN AUBADE[70]

i.

Early pre-dawn mornings, a brief
            wind thumbing through coral bell
                        vine, the tea drowsy with
                                    sweet.

Father in the kitchen, eating eggs quickly—
            the sun rising, pressing
the sin of eating
            onto his hands and feet.

ii.

The painted star. Its solid center,
            wet unseeing on my back—
                        my eyes opened, the star
                                    briefly
                                                spinning.

69. *amar naam Tarfia*: (Bangla) "My name is Tarfia."

70. *Ramadan*: The month during which daytime fasting is observed in Islam. *Aubade*: A song or poem to greet the dawn; often a love poem.

iii.

No, not another bite, I say.
      Bananas soaked in milk.
Coconuts shaved into
            moon-
    curls.

iv.

Hours on the prayer mat.
    I wanted to be sacrosanct,
              rubbed clean, new palimpsest[71]
folded—
    narrower and narrower threads of hunger.

v.

Later, I tried to sing myself into fire,
    but became a knife instead.
        The center held briefly, then broke into
        a wall of wine-red doorways.

71. *palimpsest*: A parchment on which writing has been erased and written over.

Hannah Faith Notess
(b. 1981)

FRIDAY

Maybe the prisoner's mother
didn't block her ears against
the swinging whip, the dragging
chain, the buzz of voltage
that set off fireworks in the brain.
Maybe she has strength to hold

his body one more time, once
it is finished. And maybe the body
is a darkness into which we must
keep looking. But there is more
pain already on this earth
than most of us can bear.

Why should we look
upon the same splayed form
so often that we notice only
how bony his knees are
in one painting, how taut
the skin of his pierced side

in another? Take him down
and let his mother hold him.
Let him be buried, let
the story's pages turn. And when
the earth splits, when the veil
is torn, when the dead stumble

dazed from the tombs, trailing
their moldy bandages behind them,
let the thunderclap announce
that agony flows only outward
from broken blood vessels,
no longer settling in the soul.

SUNDAY

In the garden, a girl waits
for what she has seen to make sense.
It was too early, hardly light.
And the clouds had not parted,
no ray of sun had lit the water
beaded in the spiderwebs
to weave them into a glittering shawl.

In the garden, the girl remembers
the room felt as though someone
had just walked out, and it smelled
not of incense, but of earth,
not of balm or spices, but the rust
in the clay that tastes of blood.

In the garden, she listens
to the steady drop of rain on leaf.
And as the wind unfurls the sweet
breath of stem and petal,
the garden begins to smell
like the kingdom of heaven.

In the garden, no one will ask her
to give up grief altogether,
not yet. But a man will say
her name, as though her name
could answer any question,

and she will say nothing to anyone
because what she has seen
is cold and clear as water
running over the hands of a blind girl
before she was made to see.

Malachi Black
(b. 1982)

FROM "Quarantine"[72]

Sext

I have known you as an opening
of curtains as a light blurts through
the sky. But this is afternoon
and afternoon is not the time

to hunt you with the hot globe
of a human eye. So I fluster
like a crooked broom in rounds
within the living room, and try
to lift an ear to you. I try.

I cut myself into a cave for you.
To be a trilling blindness
in the infinite vibration
of your murmuring July,
I cut myself into a cave for you.

Vespers

My Lord, you are the one:
your breath has blown away
            the visionary sun
and now suffocates the skyline
            with a dusk. If only once,
I wish that you could shudder
with my pulse,   double over
and convulse   on the stitches
in the skin that I slash wishes in.
            But, Lord, you are the gulf
between the hoped-for
                  and the happening:
You've won. So what is left for me
when what is left for me has come?

---

72. According to the author, "Cast as a crown of sonnets, the ten movements of 'Quarantine' derive their logic and arrangement from the Christian monastic prayer cycle known generally as the canonical hours (*horae canonicae*). 'Quarantine' traces the passage of one day, from predawn prayer ('Lauds') through sunrise ('Prime'), morning ('Terce'), midday ('Sext'), afternoon ('None'), sundown ('Vespers'), night ('Nocturne'), midnight ('Vigils'), and concludes at early morning ('Matins')."

Matins

The floating endlessly again:
the glowing and the growing back
again as I am as I can and I can stand.
I understand.
              Though I am fashioned
in the haggard image of a man,
I am an atom of the aperture.

I am as a nerve inside a gland.

I understand. Though I am fashioned
as I am, I am a perch for the eternal
and a purse for what it lends.
I understand.
              Though flakes of fire
overwhelm the fallen snow, though ice
caps melt, though oceans freeze or overflow,
somehow I am sturdier, more sure.

Nate Klug
(b. 1985)

DARE

Not, this time, to infer
but to wait you out
between regret and parking lot
somewhere in the day
like a dare

Salt grime and the foodcarts'
rising steam, at Prospect St. a goshawk
huge and aloof, picking at something,
nested in twigs and police tape
For a while we all
held our phones up

It is relentless, the suddenness
of every other
song, creature, neighbor
as though this life
would prove you
only by turning into itself

Ashley Anna McHugh
(b. 1985)

ONE IMPORTANT AND ELEGANT PROOF

> Joseph:
> *How am I then to know,*
> *Father, that you are just?*
> *Give me one reason?*
>
> Gabriel:
> *No.*
>
> –W. H. Auden, from *For The Time Being*

"This isn't something that I thought I'd do.
People just kept on telling me I should."

The clock.

      Lips stiff, he let her pause. No question.
She thought he was supposed to ask her questions.
"People kept on telling me I should.
That's all, you know? So. Here I am. That's all."

"And why would people tell you that?"

                    "Don't know."
The clock.   *The clock.*

      His pencil on the pad.
Scrape of the lead. She talked to stop him writing.

"I'm just OK. Not good, not bad. OK."

The clock.

     "OK as anyone, I guess."

"Why just OK?"
      "Don't know." He tapped his pencil.
She thought that he might ask a question. No.

He let her pause.

        The clock.   *The clock.*   *The clock.*

"I grew up Christian, thinking things made sense.
You know? To someone. God? If not to me."
She thought
             that he might ask a question. No.
She sat up straighter in the silence.
                        Swallowed.
"My father's Protestant, my mother's Catholic.
But neither practices. I'm not religious,
not really—but one time, when I was living
in Vermont, I went to Sunday mass. I think
on a feast day, one for Saint Joseph maybe.
Who knows? But I was sitting near the front
when these boys, about a half a dozen maybe,
came walking up the aisle, swinging censers—
and as they passed, the people toward the back
just started crying, pew by pew. These strangers,
in tears. Not sobbing hard—for the most part
they all kept quiet—except for here and there
I'd hear somebody groan, all soft. I tried
to mind my business, keep my nose to myself,
but I caught myself just staring at one family.
I couldn't stop. The father looked embarrassed,
wouldn't touch the tears, like they weren't there.
Just let them run into his beard. I watched
his wife. Her lips were moving, muttering
—maybe a prayer? She kept on looking up,
blinking, and then running the side of her finger
under her eyes until mascara streaked it.
This red–faced little girl hung on her elbow,
rubbing her face against her mother's arm.
Then I heard this sigh, a rattle of a sigh,
and turned. The teenage boy right next to me
was biting his lip, his fingers digging hard
into the pew. And then he started, too.
His sister—girlfriend?—crumpled down. Just sat,
twisting and untwisting the hem of her dress.
Trying to focus on something else, I guess.
But then the boys walked past, expressionless,
and I cried like everyone—no reason at all,
no hope or fear or pain to speak of, cried
for nothing."
               She waited for a question. No.

She tried to think of something else to say.
"I don't know why. I guess—." He let her pause.
She saw his pencil hadn't moved. Why not?
He twisted the band of his watch.

> *The clock.   The clock.*

She knew she ought to talk. "I guess I think
Maybe the ritual of it had moved me?
Or maybe God was really there? Or else
the Holy Spirit? Something. Maybe not.
It was a visceral response, almost.
Simple. Simple is just the only word."
He let her pause. His pencil tapped the pad.
She tried to think of something else to say.
Opened, closed her mouth.

> *The clock.   The clock.*

He lifted his wrist. "We made some progress here,
I think. Enough for tonight." No question. No
advice. No nothing. She didn't move to leave.
"Next Wednesday, then?" And she caught her face in her hands.
"I've got you down for Wednesday. Six o'clock."

He stood. He turned a knob. She didn't move.
He lifted his wrist. She didn't move to leave.
She didn't leave. Doorway. Florescent hall.
She hoped that he would ask her anything.

Waited.

> *The clock.   The clock.   The clock.   The clock.*

ALL OTHER GROUND IS SINKING SAND

Thine be the kingdom and the power and the glory.
He's paralyzed, so it's common: his bedsore.
But my father prays for himself, he tells this Bible story:

Cripple lowered from the roof into the flurry
around Jesus; healed, he climbed up off the floor.
Thine be the kingdom and the power and the glory.

On the stove, Dakin Solution hisses, boils. We worry
the wound. Twice every day, and sometimes more:

green gauze changed out. His Bible opens to this story:

Take up thy bed, and walk. No prayer. No oratory,
but the cripple's muscles flexed: like never before,
they moved, and he stood. *Thine the power, and the glory.*

Doctors say that he could die: They have to hurry,
might amputate. He's still, then the click of the door,
and my father cries, he prays—but this is a hard story:

Staph spreads, and surgeons treat his body like a quarry.
Close to his spine, they mine the green-black ore—
and still, he prays. I can't—but this is my father's story.
So, Thine be the kingdom. Thine, the power. Thine, the glory.

Anna Connors
(b. 1991)

HANGING

Hanging, feet hooked over the monkey-bars,
I used to listen for the Lord.
I waited until my ears hummed with blood
and blue reached my lips and under my eyes.
I was closer to the ground than I expected
when I did fall—relieved.

I tried it time after time
and I still believe, or pretend, those red moments
were somehow holy—
my corn-yellow hair strewn like hayseed,
the latent Messiah come, as wind, to hum
and blow across my gravel-pocked feet.

I learned to chase, to reach for others with my fingertips.
I have followed them through their homes
and I say I too am chained to this world,
trammeled like an animal to this town.
The mobbing clouds look like sheep
in this slant of day and wildly run.

Don't ask me to reach within myself and search
for something sounding like an answer.
I don't want to distinguish what I touch.
Let me ask someone else, "What is this?"
(What piece of obsidian has been pulled
from my body's fallow land?)

I am the self-mutilating parakeet
a child kept and loved.
When I hear my owner's voice,
I can suddenly feel my wings.
I slap them against the bars.
I dismantle my persimmon-brown feathers.

Anna Connors

My body claps against metal,
A tongue in an accidental bell.
Push me, Lord, I swing.
I still sing. But maybe one night I will forget
the slow, low, humming sound

I once heard as a child hanging.
Or maybe everything
will begin to sound like it.

Appendix

An Interview with Luke Hankins[1]

by Justin Bigos

Justin Bigos: Your first book of poems, *Weak Devotions*, contains a fifteen-part sequence of the same title. The sequence as well as the book contains much conversation with God, often interrogating His motives—even His very authority. What is the human cost of entering this mysterious place of devotion—as God once entered the mystery of "mortal flesh," "his holiest act"? Is a "weak devotion" the closest we humans come to something holy?

Luke Hankins: Yehuda Amichai writes in his poem "Relativity"[2]:

> Someone told me he's going down to Sinai because
> he wants to be alone with his God:
> I warned him.

Indeed.

You ask what the human cost of entering "the mysterious place of devotion" is. In my experience, it is very high. And judging by what poets devoted to God throughout the ages have written, I think they would agree. But I don't think anyone enters a devout life counting the cost—not even monastics and ascetics (which I certainly have never been). That's because one can't imagine or begin to comprehend the actual price until it's already being exacted. Hopkins, in "Carrion Comfort," writes:

> But ah, but O thou terrible, why wouldst thou rude on me
> Thy wring-world right foot rock? lay a lionlimb against me?

The psalmist(s) of Psalm 42 write(s):

> Deep calls to deep
> in the roar of your waterfalls;
> all your waves and breakers
> have swept over me.

1. This interview originally appeared on the *American Literary Review* blog: http://americanliter-aryreview.blogspot.com.

2. See pp. 38 & 39 of this volume.

Some, from a perspective outside of religious or spiritual devotion, would undoubtedly say that the cost is high because the devout are fooling themselves, chasing after shadows and myths and confronting their own neuroses in the dark, working themselves into a frenzy seeking what was never there to begin with. This is certainly not a novel idea for anyone who has ever genuinely sought the divine. (E.g., see R. S. Thomas's poem "Threshold."[3]) Whom do you meet in the desert? Is it the Maker in whom you see all of your fears and all of your hopes embodied, or is it the Nothing in which you see only a reflection of your own inexplicable being? And which is more terrifying?

But though the cost of entering this desert is undoubtedly high, you come away changed irrevocably—which may be worth having experienced that "dark night of the soul." As Andrew Marvell writes in "The Definition of Love":

> Magnanimous Despair alone
>   Could show me so divine a thing,
> Where feeble Hope could ne'er have flown,
>   But vainly flapped its tinsel wing.

I grew up in an evangelical, conservative Christian environment, and I clung desperately to that faith for most of my life, through constant cycles of doubt and belief. *Weak Devotions*, and particularly the title poem, chronicles the doubt and belief that has always been interwoven in my life, and more recently the evolution away from traditional religious beliefs toward—what?—a deeper acknowledgment of mystery and uncertainty. This, for me, was a very traumatic transition, in which I felt that my framework for understanding life was torn away, leaving me floating in a void. This spiritual transition coincided with a year-long period of intense and unremitting anxiety, a psychological problem I've dealt with since early childhood that suddenly burst out of control, and a mercifully shorter period of depression—a depth I hope to never touch again with so much as my little toe.

I realize that to write poems about this subject risks alienating any readers who have no experience with a religious upbringing or—more to the point—with primal and deep-seated religious beliefs of their own. My hope in this respect is that something like what T. S. Eliot has said about George Herbert's poetry might prove true of poetry like mine as well (not to in any way compare the quality of my poems with that of Herbert's!):

> When I claim a place for Herbert among those poets whose work every lover
> of English poetry should read and every student of English poetry should
> study, irrespective of religious belief or unbelief, I am not thinking primarily
> of the exquisite craftsmanship, the extraordinary metrical virtuosity, or the

---

3. See pp. 20 & 21 of this volume.

verbal felicities, but of the *content* of the poems which make up *The Temple*. These poems form a record of spiritual struggle which should touch the feeling, and enlarge the understanding of those readers also who hold no religious belief and find themselves unmoved by religious emotion. (italics Eliot's)[4]

Finally, you ask whether a "weak devotion" is the closest we as humans may come to something holy. My response is that we as humans do not come to what is holy at all. In my (of course subjective) experience, I see the opposite as true: the holy comes to us, and we can never be ready for it. (The holy is always *other*—etymologically, the word implies that which is whole, complete, inviolate—unlike us.) Our weak devotion is a reaction more than it is an action. In the poem of mine you quote, I do write of entering into mystery, but that is in itself a response to a prompting from outside. Those who enter the desert do not do it of their own volition, but are driven there by the wind of the Spirit. If it were up to us, I think none of us would ever go. We don't want the terror, the pain, the annihilation of the self. But it seems that the Holy sees fit to drive some to that point—not all, and perhaps not even many. Why this is, I couldn't say. I happen to believe that the will behind this is beneficent, only because of having come through my small version of the experience. Had you asked me during the most trying periods, you would have been met with silence, or worse. But now, like Marvell, I do in my better moments believe despair to be magnanimous.

JB: For such a serious book, I love when your strange humor arrives, such as in the poem "Portrait of Myself as a Barbarian." The poem exists in "some barbarous century / long before the invention / of eyeglasses," and the speaker makes his way through the world, laughing, even as the unseen wolves advance. I thought I was the only one with the private fantasy/fear of living in a time without corrective lenses, since my vision is horrible. The poem pleases me with its vulnerability and fortitude, and I wonder if it's between those two things that humor sometimes appears. So: can we bring humor to the table when having our sit–downs with God?

LH: You mention humor in "our sit-downs with God," and I immediately think of the character Tevye in the musical "Fiddler on the Roof." What a marvelous example of humor in conversation with the divine! Well, Tevye's kind of humor requires a nonchalance and self-confidence that I don't naturally possess. But there are so many kinds of humor, and perhaps the one I most appreciate in poetry arises from the kind of irony we see in Emily Dickinson, W. H. Auden, Elizabeth Bishop, or, more recently, Kay Ryan, in which a grave subject is spoken of in a relatively lighthearted way, which can paradoxically increase the emotional impact of the poem once the

4. Eliot, T. S. "George Herbert as Religious Poet." In *George Herbert and the Seventeenth-century Religious Poets*, edited by Mario A. di Cesare, 239. New York: W. W. Norton, 1978.

serious underpinnings of the humor are recognized. I hope to include more poems with this kind of humor in my next book, which is in progress under the title *Ex Nihilo*—a very serious, Latin title! Here's one small example of the kind of humor I'm talking about in one of my newer poems, in its entirety:

> On Judgment
>
> In canine mythology,
> Sisyphus is the most blessèd of all,
> granted an eternal game of fetch.

The humor of a dog's perspective on mythology, and on the myth of Sisyphus in particular, is obvious. But I hope that the poem also works on a deeper level, in which it comments on the way one's perspective and state of mind can make hell of heaven and heaven of hell—the way that what we now view as a curse we might one day learn to see as a blessing.

JB: One of my favorite poems in the book is the villanelle "A Shape with Forty Wings," which will appear in the next issue of *American Literary Review*. I'm curious how long it took you to write this poem. I have tried many villanelles over the years, and I have never written a good one. Do you need to have strong repeating lines right away, or can those come later? (Your terrific repeating lines are: "Love is strange and calls me to stranger things" and "I've drawn my life—a shape with forty wings.")

LH: As with most of my poems, I wrote the initial poem fairly quickly, then over a period of several years came back to it and revised it numerous times. In this case, the refrains came first. I think that it's helpful to have a meter in mind if you decide to come up with refrain lines first, so that instead of pulling words out of thin air you at least have some sort of framework—a length of utterance, at least—to drop them into. Here, it's pentameter, but there are no restrictions on which meter is required in a villanelle, though pentameter has historically been a favorite in English-language villanelles.

But there is no right or wrong way to compose a poem, whether free verse or "formal." We all work on finding what works for us—and of course what worked for us once or a dozen times may not work for the next poem, and we may have to try new strategies. The important thing is to be willing to be flexible, and once you have something on the page, to be able to achieve a level of objectivity in assessing its success or lack thereof.

JB: I know you have spoken and written about this before, including on NPR, but I wonder if you'd be willing to discuss yet one more time the assault you suffered last summer. For readers who don't know: you were assaulted by four people in July of 2011; the perpetrators called you "faggot" and made fun of the way you were dressed, and they did not attempt to steal your money or car. This was clearly a hate crime. The attack took place in Asheville, North Carolina, a city that prides itself on its liberal—and especially pro-gay—values. You've written a poem, "The Way They Loved Each Other,"[5] about the event, and one of the things I admire about it is that the speaker recognizes a love in the attackers, even if "tribal," "primal." But I also admire that you were able to write such a gracious poem so quickly after the event. People sometimes make fun of poetry that seems written as therapy, but what else can a poem like yours do but attempt to heal—both yourself and the world? Are people unfair when they mock the poem of therapy, or is there a difference between therapy and art?

LH: The difficulty with comparing art and therapy is on one level merely a semantic one: we have certain associations with the sterile and history-laden word "therapy" that we are—rightly, I suppose—loath to bring into a conversation about art. Art—indeed, beauty itself—is perennially therapeutic. We might prefer the terms restorative, or calming, or invigorating, or pleasure-inducing, or any number of terms that indicate the very real physiological and psychological effects of the aesthetic experience of objects, sounds, and ideas. But regardless of how we describe it, it's true that we often change for the better through our aesthetic experiences. I know beyond a shadow of a doubt that this has been true for me—so much so that the word "therapy" is quite reductive.

Writing the poem about the assault I experienced was primarily an attempt on my part to understand those who had attacked me, and by doing so to understand what seemed to me an inexplicable event. You're right that the assailants didn't try to steal anything. They apparently had no motive other than to hurt someone they perceived as different from themselves. And that was the most difficult aspect of the event to deal with. It filled me with inexpressible sorrow and anxiety, not only for myself but also for them. The pain of the fractured bones in my face was intense, but my inability to comprehend why or how these people could have acted this way was by far the more traumatizing aspect. I was sad not only for my experience, but for the lives of the people who had chosen to do this to me. What must their lives be like for this to be how they spent their time? But by making something out of the confusion and pain, I felt that I was able to redeem the experience and instead of dwelling on how it had hurt me or how inexplicable others' actions were, I attempted to come to an understanding of their actions as human, as not other but as familiar. Joseph Conrad has said something marvelous in his famous "Preface":

---

5. "The Way They Loved Each Other" can be read on the blog of the American Public Media program *On Being* at http://blog.onbeing.org/post/8640670635/.

> [The artist] speaks to our capacity for delight and wonder, to the sense of mystery surrounding our lives; to our sense of pity, and beauty, and pain; to the latent feeling of fellowship with all creation—and to the subtle but invincible conviction of solidarity that knits together the loneliness of innumerable hearts: to the solidarity in dreams, in joy, in sorrow, in aspirations, in illusions, in hope, in fear, which binds men to each other, which binds together all humanity—the dead to the living and the living to the unborn.[6]

Making art is essential to who we are as humans—we are artificers, makers, shapers. And through shaping words or paint or musical notes many of us sense that we are fully engaging with what it means to be human—and we are able to come to a fuller understanding of what it means for others to be human as well—a conviction of what Conrad calls our "solidarity."

In the Christian tradition, humans are made "in the image of God,"[7] and since God is the great Maker, we as reflections of the divine are also makers. For me this is one of the most beautiful and most essential Christian teachings. We make because we are made. We are made because God loves to make. We are the result of the pleasureful work of the divine. And we sense this most, perhaps, when we are ourselves engaged in the pleasureful work of making art.

6. Conrad, Joseph. "Preface." In *The Nigger of the 'Narcissus'*, 11–16. Garden City, NY: Doubleday, 1914.

7. See Genesis 1:27.

Biographies

Malaika King Albrecht's (b. 1965) first full-length book of poems, *What the Trapeze Artist Trusts*, was published by Press 53 in 2012. Her chapbook *Lessons in Forgetting* was published by Main Street Rag and was a finalist in the 2011 Next Generation Indie Book Awards and received honorable mention for the 2011 Brockman-Campbell Award. Her latest chapbook, *Spill*, was also published by Main Street Rag. Her poems have been published in many literary magazines and anthologies and are translated into several languages, including Farsi and Hindi. Her poems have recently won awards at the North Carolina Poetry Council, Salem College, and Press 53. Albrecht the founding editor of *Redheaded Stepchild*, an online magazine that only accepts poems that have been rejected elsewhere. She lives in Pinehurst, NC with her family and is a therapeutic riding instructor.

Agha Shahid Ali (1949–2001) was born in New Delhi and grew up Muslim in Kashmir. He earned a Ph.D. in English from Pennsylvania State University in 1984, and an M.F.A. from the University of Arizona in 1985. His volumes of poetry include *Call Me Ishmael Tonight: A Book of Ghazals* (W.W. Norton, 2003), *Rooms Are Never Finished* (2001), *The Country Without a Post Office* (1997), and *The Beloved Witness: Selected Poems* (1992). He is also the editor of *Ravishing Disunities: Real Ghazals in English* (2000). Among Ali's many honors was a fellowship from the Guggenheim Foundation. He taught at many schools, including the University of Delhi, Penn State, SUNY Binghamton, Princeton University, Hamilton College, Baruch College, University of Utah, and Warren Wilson College.

Yehuda Amichai (1924–2000) was born in Wurzburg, Germany, and emigrated to Palestine with his family in 1936. Amichai has published eleven volumes of poetry in Hebrew, two novels, and a book of short stories. His work has been translated into thirty-seven languages. In 1982 he received the Israel Prize for Poetry and in 1986 he became a foreign honorary member of the American Academy of Arts and Letters. Amichai lived in Jerusalem until September 2000, when he died of cancer.

A. (Archie) R. (Randolph) Ammons (1926–2001) grew up on a tobacco farm near Whiteville, North Carolina. Ammons published his first book of poems, *Ommateum: With Doxology*, in 1955. He subsequently published nearly thirty collections, including *Bosh and Flapdoodle* (2005), *Glare* (1997), *Garbage* (1993), *A Coast of Trees* (1981), *Sphere* (1974), and *Collected Poems 1951–1971* (1972). His honors and awards include two National Book Awards (in 1973, for *Collected Poems 1951–1971*, and in 1993, for *Garbage*); a 1981 National Book Critics Circle Award for *A Coast of Trees*; a 1993 Library of Congress Rebekah Johnson Bobbitt National Prize for

Poetry for *Garbage*; a 1971 Bollingen Prize for *Sphere*; the Academy of American Poet's Wallace Stevens Award; the Poetry Society of America's Robert Frost Medal; the Ruth Lilly Prize; and fellowships from the Guggenheim Foundation, the MacArthur Foundation, and the American Academy of Arts and Letters. Ammons taught at Cornell University from 1964 until his retirement in 1988. During his time there he became the Goldwin Smith Professor of English and Poet in Residence. He lived in Ithaca, New York until his death.

Bruce Beasley (b. 1958) grew up in Macon, Georgia. He is the author *Theophobia*, forthcoming from BOA Editions, as well as six other collections of poetry. He is the recipient of numerous awards, including the 1993 Ohio State University Press/*The Journal* Award, the 1996 Colorado Prize for Poetry, the 2005 Georgia Press' Contemporary Poetry Series Award, a fellowship from the National Endowment for the Arts, and three Pushcart Prizes in poetry. He currently lives and teaches in Bellingham, Washington, where he is a Professor of English at Western Washington University.

Wendell Berry (b. 1934) was born in New Castle, Kentucky. He attended the University of Kentucky at Lexington where he received a B.A. in English in 1956 and an M.A. in 1957. Berry is the author of more than thirty books of poetry, essays, and novels. His collections of poetry include *Given* (2005), *A Timbered Choir: The Sabbath Poems 1979–1997* (1997), and *The Selected Poems of Wendell Berry* (1988). His novels include *Jayber Crow* (2001), *A World Lost* (1996), and *Remembering* (1988). Berry is also the author of *Imagination in Place* (2011), *The Unsettling of America: Culture & Agriculture* (2004), *Another Turn of the Crank* (1995), *Sex, Economy, Freedom, & Community* (1993), *Standing on Earth: Selected Essays* (1991), and *A Continuous Harmony: Essays Cultural and Agricultural* (1972). He has taught at New York University and at the University of Kentucky. He has received fellowships from the Guggenheim and Rockefeller Foundations, a Lannan Foundation Award, and a grant from the National Endowment for the Arts. He lives on a farm in Port Royal, Kentucky.

John Berryman (1914–1972) was born John Smith in McAlester, Oklahoma. When Berryman was twelve, his father committed suicide, shooting himself outside the boy's window. This traumatic event darkened the rest of Berryman's life. His mother re-married and John took his step-father's name, Berryman. He attended Columbia College and Cambridge University. Known as an excellent teacher, Berryman taught at various schools, including Harvard, Princeton, and the University of Minnesota. He began to attract widespread attention as a poet with his 1956 volume *Homage to Mistress Bradstreet*, and his innovative and most well-known work, *The Dream Songs*, served to increase his acclaim and seal his reputation as one of the most essential American poets of his era. Berryman never recovered from the trauma of his father's suicide, and he suffered from emotional instability and alcoholism throughout his life. In 1972, he committed suicide by throwing himself off a bridge in Minneapolis.

Justin Bigos (b. 1975) was born in New Haven, Connecticut. He has studied writing at Carnegie Mellon University, the Warren Wilson M.F.A. Program for Writers, and the University of North Texas, where he is currently a Ph.D. candidate. His poems have appeared in magazines including *The Gettysburg Review*, *Ploughshares*, *Indiana Review*, *Crazyhorse*, and *The Collagist*.

Malachi Black (b. 1982) is the author of *Storm Toward Morning*, forthcoming from Copper Canyon Press, and two limited-edition chapbooks: *Quarantine* (Argos Books, 2012) and *Echolocation* (Float Press, 2010). His work has appeared in journals including *Poetry*, *Boston Review*, *Blackbird*, *Harvard Review*, and *Gulf Coast*, among others, and in several recent anthologies, including *Discoveries: New Writing from the Iowa Review* (2012). The recipient of a 2009 Ruth Lilly Fellowship from Poetry magazine and the Poetry Foundation, he has also received fellowships from the Fine Arts Work Center in Provincetown, The MacDowell Colony, the University of Texas at Austin's Michener Center for Writers, and the University of Utah. He was the John Atherton Scholar at the 2010 Bread Leaf Writers' Conference, and was the subject of an emerging poet profile by Mark Jarman in the Fall 2011 issue of the Academy of American Poets' *American Poet* magazine.

Josephy Brodsky (1940–1996) was born in Leningrad and began writing poetry at age eighteen. Having left school at age fifteen, Brodsky was sentenced to five years of hard labor for "social parasitism," but he only served 18 months of his term. He was exiled from the Soviet Union in 1972, but before leaving studied with the celebrated Russian poet Anna Akhmatova, who recognized in him a rare and powerful lyrical gift. He then moved to the United States, living in Brooklyn and Massachusetts. Brodsky came to be known as the greatest Russian poet of his generation and wrote nine volumes of poetry, as well as several collections of essays, and received the Nobel Prize for Literature in 1987. In addition to teaching positions at Columbia University and Mount Holyoke College, where he taught for fifteen years, Brodsky served as Poet Laureate of the United States from 1991 to 1992. Brodsky died in 1996 of a heart attack.

Jericho Brown (b. 1976) worked as the speechwriter for the Mayor of New Orleans before receiving his Ph.D. in Creative Writing and Literature from the University of Houston. He also holds an M.F.A. from the University of New Orleans and a B.A. from Dillard University. The recipient of the Whiting Writers Award and fellowships from the National Endowment for the Arts, the Radcliffe Institute at Harvard University, the Bread Loaf Writers' Conference, and the Krakow Poetry Seminar in Poland, Brown is an Assistant Professor at the University of San Diego. His poems have appeared in journals and anthologies including *The American Poetry Review*, *The Believer*, *jubilat*, *Oxford American*, *Ploughshares*, *A Public Space*, and *100 Best African American Poems*. His first book, *Please* (New Issues), won the American Book Award.

Biographies

Steven C. Brown Jr. (b. 1980) is an internationally published author whose work engages poetry, photography, and Utopian Studies. Recent publications include a volume of poetry coupled with photographs by Jerry Uelsmann titled, *Moth and Bonelight* (21st Editions, 2010); an essay on utopias and gardens in *Earth Perfect? Nature, Utopia and the Garden* (London: Black Dog, 2012); and three books forthcoming by the German publisher Edition Galerie Vevais on photographers whose works coincide with Brown's utopian interests. Brown is currently pursuing his Ph.D. at Harvard in the History of American Civilization.

Scott Cairns (b. 1954) was born in Tacoma, Washington. He has published six collections of poetry, including *Compass of Affection: Poems New and Selected* (2006); a spiritual memoir; and a collection of translations of texts by Christian mystics. Cairns has taught at Kansas State University, Westminster College, University of North Texas, Old Dominion University, and currently holds positions as Professor of English and Director of Creative Writing at the University of Missouri. He was awarded a Guggenheim fellowship in 2006.

Richard Chess (b. 1953) is the author of three books of poetry, *Third Temple* (2007), *Chair in the Desert* (2000), and *Tekiah* (1994). His poems have appeared in many journals as well as several anthologies, including *Bearing the Mystery: 25 Years of Image*, *Best American Spiritual Writing 2005*, and *Telling and Remembering: A Century of American–Jewish Poetry*. An award winning teacher, he is the Roy Carroll Professor of Honors Arts and Sciences and Professor of Literature and Language at the University of North Carolina at Asheville. He directs UNCA's Center for Jewish Studies. He has been a member of the low–residency M.F.A. faculties at Warren Wilson College and Queens College and he served for a number of years as writer–in–residence at the Brandeis Bardin Institute in Simi Valley, California. He also served as assistant director of The Jewish Arts Institute at Elat Chayyim, located at the Isabella Freedman Retreat Center, where he taught creative writing in a two–year training institute. Having completed the Jewish Mindfulness Teacher Training Program, he is a co-leader of the Asheville Jewish Mindfulness Meditation Circle at Congregation Beth Israel. He is also working to introduce, encourage, and provide support for the use of contemplative pedagogy at UNC Asheville and other educational institutions.

Leonard Cohen (b. 1934) was born in Montreal and attended McGill University. He is a renowned songwriter and author who, over the course of half a century, has published numerous books of poetry, including *Stranger Music: Selected Poems and Songs* (Vintage Books, 1994); two novels; and almost twenty records, including *Various Positions*, *I'm Your Man*, and *Old Ideas*.

Anna Connors (b. 1991) will complete B.A. degrees in English and psychology at Indiana University, Bloomington in 2013. She plans to enter a Ph.D. program in organizational theory and behavior. She has had a poem published in *Asheville Poetry Review*.

Robert Cording (b. 1949) teaches English and creative writing at College of the Holy Cross, where he is the Barrett Professor of Creative Writing. He has published six collections of poems: *Life-list*, which won the Ohio State University Press/*The Journal* award in 1987; *What Binds Us To This World* (Copper Beech Press, 1991); *Heavy Grace* (Alice James, 1996); *Against Consolation* (CavanKerry Press, 2002); *Common Life*, (CavanKerry Press, 2006); and his newest, *Walking With Ruskin* (CavanKerry, 2010). He has received two National Endowment for the Arts fellowships in poetry and two poetry grants from the Connecticut Commission of the Arts. His poems have appeared in numerous publications, such as *The Nation, Georgia Review, The Southern Review, Poetry, Kenyon Review, New England Review, Orion*, and *The New Yorker*.

Morri Creech (b. 1970) was born in Moncks Corner, South Carolina. He is the recipient of the 1999 Louisiana Division of the Arts Artist Fellowship, the 1997 Ruth Lilly Fellowship for Young Poets, and a 1998 Pushcart Prize nomination. His poems have appeared in *Poetry, The New Criterion, The New Republic, The Southwest Review, The Hudson Review, Crazyhorse, Critical Quarterly, Sewanee Review, The Southern Review*, and elsewhere. He has published two collections of poetry, and currently teaches at Queens University in Charlotte, NC.

E. (Edward) E. (Estlin) Cummings (b. 1894) was born in Cambridge, Massachusetts. He is one of the most beloved American poets of the 20th century, as well as a painter, essayist, author, and playwright. Cummings published thirteen collections of poetry, and was the recipient of numerous honors, including two Guggenheim fellowships, the Charles Eliot Norton Professorship at Harvard University (he also received both his A.B. and A.M. from Harvard), the 1958 Bollingen Prize in poetry, and a Ford Foundation grant. At the time of his death in 1964, Cummings was the second only to Robert Frost as the most widely read poet in the United States.

Patrice de la Tour du Pin (1911–1975) was a major French, Catholic poet of the mid-twentieth century. As a poet, he achieved fame for individual collections of poems as well as *Une Somme de poésie*, a three-volume multi-genred work he wrote and continually revised throughout his life. Late in his career, de la Tour du Pin distilled and collected his most powerful lyrical poems, written in the form of psalms, into *Psaumes de tous mes temps* [*Psalms of All My Days*]. These psalms articulate his struggle to find poetic authority and spiritual meaning in the midst of world war and modern tumult. A book of Jennifer Grotz's English translations of poems by de la Tour du Pin, *The Psalms of All My Days*, is forthcoming from Carnegie Mellon University Press in 2013.

Madeline DeFrees (b. 1919) was born in Ontario, Oregon. She served as a Catholic nun for thirty-eight years, leaving the order in 1973. She received an M.A. from the University of Oregon, and has taught at Holy Names College, University of Montana–Missoula, and University of Massachusetts–Amherst. She has published poetry collections, essays, reviews, and short stories. DeFrees has received fellowships from the Guggenheim Foundation and the National Endowment for the Arts.

Biographies

Patrick Donnelly (b. 1956) is the author of *The Charge* (Ausable Press, 2003, now part of Copper Canyon Press) and *Nocturnes of the Brothel of Ruin* (Four Way Books, 2012). He is director of the Advanced Seminar at The Frost Place, an associate editor of *Poetry International*, a contributing editor of *Trans-Portal*, and he has taught writing at Colby College, the Lesley University M.F.A. Program, the Bread Loaf Writers' Conference, and elsewhere. His poems have appeared in *American Poetry Review*, *Slate*, *Ploughshares*, *The Yale Review*, *The Virginia Quarterly Review*, and many other journals. With Stephen D. Miller, Donnelly is co-translator of the Japanese poems in *The Wind from Vulture Peak: The Buddhification of Japanese Waka in the Heian Period* (Cornell East Asia Series, 2012). Donnelly and Miller's translations have appeared in *Bateau*, *Cha: An Asian Literary Journal*, *Circumference*, thedrunkenboat. com, and *Like Clouds or Mists: Studies and Translations of Nō Plays of the Genpei War*, among other places. Donnelly is a 2008 recipient of an Artist Fellowship from the Massachusetts Cultural Council and is a member of the Massachusetts Poetry Outreach Project Advisory Board.

T. (Thomas) S. (Stearns) Eliot (1888–1965) was born in St. Louis, Missouri. He attended Harvard and did graduate work in philosophy at the Sorbonne, Harvard, and Merton College, Oxford. He moved to England, where he worked as a schoolmaster and a bank clerk before becoming the literary editor for the publishing house Faber & Faber, of which he later became a director. He founded and edited the influential literary journal *Criterion*. In 1927, Eliot became a British citizen and about the same time entered the Anglican Church. He received the Nobel Prize for Literature in 1948. Eliot is widely considered one of the greatest poets and critics of the 20th century. He died in London in 1965.

William Everson (b. 1912), also known as Brother Antoninus, was born in California. A pacifist, Everson worked at a lumber camp in the Northwest as a conscientious objector during World War II. He served as a Dominican lay brother from 1951 to 1971, during which time he struggled reconcile his poetic and religious vocations. Everson's poetry is often associated with pantheism, mysticism, and rhapsody, eroticism, and naturalism. Everson is the author of over 30 collections of poetry. He died in 1994.

Tarfia Faizullah (b. 1980) was born in Brooklyn, but grew up in Midland, Texas. She received a B.A. from the University of Texas at Austin and an M.F.A. in creative writing from Virginia Commonwealth University. A Kundiman fellow and a two-time Ruth Lilly finalist, she is the recipient of a Dorothy Sargent Rosenberg Prize, a Fulbright Fellowship, a Bread Loaf Writers' Conference Margaret Bridgman Scholarship, a *Ploughshares* Cohen Award, and an AWP Intro Journals Award. Her poems have appeared in numerous publications, including *Passages North*, *The Cincinnati Review*, *The Missouri Review*, *Crab Orchard Review*, *Notre Dame Review*, *The Southern Review*, *Ploughshares*, and *Poetry Daily*. A former associate editor of *blackbird: a journal of literature and the arts*, she lives in Richmond, Virginia, where she teaches creative writing and edits the journal *trans-portal*.

Louise Glück (b. 1943) was born in New York City and grew up on Long Island. She is the author of numerous books of poetry, including *A Village Life: Poems* (2009); *Averno*(2006), a finalist for the National Book Award in Poetry; *The Seven Ages* (2001); *Vita Nova* (1999), winner of *Boston Book Review*'s Bingham Poetry Prize and *The New Yorker*'s Book Award in Poetry; *Meadowlands* (1996); *The Wild Iris* (1992), which received the Pulitzer Prize and the Poetry Society of America's William Carlos Williams Award; *Ararat* (1990), which received the Library of Congress's Rebekah Johnson Bobbitt National Prize for Poetry; and *The Triumph of Achilles* (1985), which received the National Book Critics Circle Award, the Boston Globe Literary Press Award, and the Poetry Society of America's Melville Kane Award. She has also published a collection of essays, *Proofs and Theories: Essays on Poetry* (1994), which won the PEN/Martha Albrand Award for Nonfiction. Her honors include the Bollingen Prize in Poetry, the Lannan Literary Award for Poetry, a Sara Teasdale Memorial Prize, the MIT Anniversary Medal, the Wallace Stevens Award, and fellowships from the Guggenheim Foundation, the Rockefeller Foundation, and the National Endowment for the Arts. In 1999 Glück was elected a Chancellor of the Academy of American Poets, and in the fall of 2003 she was selected as the Library of Congress's twelfth Poet Laureate Consultant in Poetry. She is a writer-in-residence at Yale University.

Jennifer Grotz (b. 1971) was born in Canyon, Texas. She attended Tulane University for undergraduate work and Indiana University and the University of Houston to complete her graduate studies. Her first book of poetry, *Cusp*, was chosen by Yusef Komunyakaa for the Bakeless Prize and was published by Houghton Mifflin in 2003. Her second book, *The Needle*, appeared from Houghton Mifflin Harcourt in 2011. A book of her translations of poems by Patrice de la Tour du Pin, *The Psalms of All My Days*, is forthcoming from Carnegie Mellon University Press. Her poems, reviews, and translations from both the French and Polish have been published and anthologized widely, including in *New England Review*, *Ploughshares*, *American Poetry Review*, and the *Best American Poetry* anthologies for 2000, 2009, and 2011. Grotz lives in Rochester, New York, where she teaches poetry and translation at the University of Rochester. She also serves as the assistant director of the Bread Loaf Writers Conference.

Seamus Heaney (b. 1939) was born and raised in Northern Ireland. He has published poetry, criticism, plays, and translations for over forty years. Heaney was awarded the Nobel Prize in Literature in 1995. He has twice been awarded the Whitbread prize, has been made a Commandeur de L'Ordre des Arts et Lettres, and received the Geoffrey Faber Memorial Prize in 1968, the E.M. Forster Award in 1975, the Golden Wreath of Poetry in 2001, and the T. S. Eliot Prize in 2006. Having been both the Harvard and Oxford Professor of Poetry, Heaney now resides in Dublin.

Anthony Hecht (1923–2004) was born in New York City. He served as an infantryman in Germany during World War II, an experience that later exerted heavy influence on his poetry. Hecht published more than 20 books of poetry, prose, and translations and served as the U.S. Poet Laureate. He received the Pulitzer Prize for

Poetry in 1968, the Bollingen Prize in 1983, the Ruth Lilly Poetry Prize in 1988, the Wallace Stevens Award in 1997, the 1999/2000 Frost Medal, the Tanning Prize, and a National Medal of Arts (awarded posthumously). Hecht was a professor for most of his life, working at a number of institutions, including Kenyon College, New York University, Bard College, Georgetown University, Harvard University, and Yale University.

Zbigniew Herbert (1924–1998) was born in Lvov, formerly eastern Poland, now a part of the Ukraine. Under German occupation, Herbert studied clandestinely at the underground King John Casimir University, where he majored in Polish literature. He was a member of the underground resistance movement. In 1944, he moved to Krakow, and three years later he graduated from the University of Krakow with a master's degree in economics. He also received a law degree from Nicholas Copernicus University in Torun and studied philosophy at the University of Warsaw under Henryk Elzenberg. He wrote numerous books of poetry, including *The Chord of Light* (1956); *Hermes, the Dog and the Star* (1957); *Study of the Object* (1961); *Mr. Cogito* (1964); and *Report from the Besieged City* (1984). His *Selected Poems*, translated into English by Czeslaw Milosz and Peter Dale Scott, was published in 1968, and most recently, *The Collected Poems: 1956–1998*, translated by Alissa Valles, was published in 2008. In 1962, Herbert published his famous collection of essays, *Barbarian in the Garden*, which was eventually translated into many languages. Herbert's awards include the Koscielski Foundation Prize, the Lenau Prize, the Alfred Jurzykowski Prize, the Herder Prize, the Petrarch Prize, the Bruno Schulz Prize, and the Jerusalem Prize. Herbert was co-editor of a poetry journal, *Poezja*, from 1965 to 1968, but he resigned in protest of anti-Semitic policies. He traveled widely through the West and lived in Paris, Berlin, and the United States, where he taught briefly at the University of California at Los Angeles.

Geoffrey Hill (b. 1932) was born in Bromsgrove, Worcestershire. He received his B.A. and M.A. from Keble College, Oxford, where he studied English literature. His collections of poetry include *Clavics* (2011); *Selected Poems* (2010); *A Treatise of Civil Power* (2008); *The Orchards of Syon* (2002); *Speech! Speech!* (2000); *The Triumph of Love* (1998), winner of the Heinemann Book Award; *Canaan* (1997), winner of the Kahn Award; *The Mystery of the Charity of Charles Péguy* (1983); *Tenebrae* (1978); *Mercian Hymns* (1971); *King Log* (1968); and *For the Unfallen* (1958). He has also published several collections of essays, journal and periodical articles, prose, and an adaptation of Henrik Ibsen's *Brand*. Hill's honors and awards include the Faber Memorial Prize, the Hawthornden Prize, the Loines Award of the American Academy and Institute of Arts and Letters, the T. S. Eliot Award for Creative Writing from the Ingersoll Foundation, and a Churchill fellowship at the University of Bristol. He is an honorary fellow of Keble College, Oxford, and Emmanuel College, Cambridge; a fellow of the Royal Society of Literature, London; and a member of the American Academy of Arts and Sciences. Hill has taught at numerous universities and is currently Professor of Poetry at the University of Oxford.

Jane Hirshfield (b. 1953) was born in New York City. After receiving her B.A. from Princeton University in their first graduating class to include women, she went on to study at the San Francisco Zen Center. Her books of poetry include *Come, Thief* (2011); *After* (2006); *Given Sugar, Given Salt* (2001); *The Lives of the Heart* (1997); *The October Palace* (1994); *Of Gravity & Angels* (1988); and *Alaya* (1982). She is also the author of *Nine Gates: Entering the Mind of Poetry* (1997) and has edited and co-translated *The Ink Dark Moon: Poems by Ono no Komachi and Izumi Shikibu, Women of the Ancient Court of Japan* (1990) with Mariko Aratani; *Mirabai: Ecstatic Poems* (2006) with Robert Bly; *Women in Praise of the Sacred: Forty-Three Centuries of Spiritual Poetry by Women* (1994); and an e-book on Basho, *The Heart of Haiku* (2011). Her honors include The Poetry Center Book Award, fellowships from the National Endowment for the Arts and Guggenheim and Rockefeller Foundations, and Columbia University's Translation Center Award. In 2004, Hirshfield was awarded the 70th Academy Fellowship for distinguished poetic achievement by The Academy of American Poets. In addition to her work as a freelance writer, editor, and translator, Hirshfield has taught in the Bennington M.F.A. Writing Seminars, at UC Berkeley, and at the University of San Francisco. She was elected Chancellor of the Academy of American Poets in 2012.

Marie Howe (b. 1950) was born in Rochester, NY. Her most recent book, *The Kingdom of Ordinary Time* (W. W. Norton, 2009) was a finalist for the Los Angeles Times Book Prize. Her other collections of poetry include *What the Living Do* (1998) and *The Good Thief* (Persea, 1988), which was selected by Margaret Atwood for the 1987 National Poetry Series. Her awards include grants from the John Simon Guggenheim Foundation, the Bunting Institute, and the National Endowment for the Arts. She has taught at Tufts University and Dartmouth College, among others. Currently she teaches at Sarah Lawrence College, New York University, and Columbia University.

Andrew Hudgins (b. 1951) was born in Killeen, Texas. He attended Huntingdon College and the University of Alabama, then earned his M.F.A. from the University of Iowa. His volumes of poetry include *American Rendering: New and Selected Poems* (2010), *Ecstatic in the Poison* (2003); *Babylon in a Jar* (1998); *The Glass Hammer: A Southern Childhood* (1994); *The Never-Ending: New Poems* (1991), a finalist for the National Book Awards; *After the Lost War: A Narrative* (1988), which received the Poetry Prize; and *Saints and Strangers* (1985), which was a finalist for the Pulitzer Prize. He is also the author of a book of essays, *The Glass Anvil* (1997). Hudgins's awards and honors include the Witter Bynner Fellowship, the Hanes Poetry Prize, and fellowships from the Bread Loaf Writers' Conference, the Ingram Merrill Foundation, and the National Endowment for the Arts. Hudgins has taught at Baylor University and University of Cincinnati; he currently teaches at Ohio State University.

Richard Jackson (b. 1946) teaches creative writing, poetry, and humanities in the University of Tennessee at Chattanooga's interdisciplinary honors program, and is a frequent guest lecturer at the M.F.A. writing seminars at Vermont College, the University of Iowa Summer Writers' Festival, and the Prague Summer Program. He is the author of ten books of poems, including *Resonance* (2010), *Half Lives:*

Petrarchan Poems (2004), and *Unauthorized Autobiography: New and Selected Poems* (2003). He has also published two books of translations: *Last Voyage: The Poems of Giovanni Pascoli* from Italian (2010) and Alexandar Persolja's *Journey of the Sun* from Slovene (2008). He is the author of two books of criticism: *Acts of Mind: Conversations with American Poets* (Choice Award) and *Dismantling Time in Contemporary Poetry* (Agee Award). He has also edited two anthologies of Slovene poetry, as well as the journal *Poetry Miscellany*. He has been awarded the Order of Freedom Medal by the President of Slovenia for literary and humanitarian work in the Balkans, and has been named a Guggenheim Fellow, Fulbright Fellow, Witter Bynner Fellow, NEA fellow, and NEH Fellow. In 2009 he was awarded the AWP George Garret National Award for Teaching and Arts Advocacy.

Mark Jarman (b. 1952) grew up in California and Scotland. He earned a B.A. from the University of California, Santa Cruz, in 1974 and an M.F.A. from the University of Iowa in 1976. His books include *Bone Fires: New and Selected Poems* (Sarabande, 2010), *Epistles* (2007), *To the Green Man* (2004), *Unholy Sonnets* (2000), *Questions for Ecclesiastes* (1997), *Iris* (1992), *The Black Riviera* (1990), *Far and Away* (1985), *The Rote Walker* (1981), and *North Sea* (1978). Jarman's awards include the Poet's Prize, the Joseph Henry Jackson Award, and fellowships from the National Endowment for the Arts and the John Simon Guggenheim Memorial Foundation. *Questions for Ecclesiastes* won the 1998 Lenore Marshall Poetry Prize and was a finalist for the National Bok Critics Circle Award. He is a Centennial Professor of English at Vanderbilt University in Nashville, Tennessee, where he lives with his wife and two daughters.

Richard Jones (b. 1953) is the author of seven books of poems, including *Apropos of Nothing*, *The Blessing*, and *The Correct Spelling & Exact Meaning*, all from Copper Canyon Press. He is Editor of the literary journal *Poetry East* and is a professor of English at DePaul University in Chicago.

Ilya Kaminsky (b. 1977) was born in Odessa, former Soviet Union. He lost most of his hearing at the age of four after a doctor misdiagnosed mumps as a cold. He arrived to the United States in 1993, when his family was granted asylum by the American government. Kaminsky earned a B.A. in political science at Georgetown University and a J.D. at the University of California's Hastings College of the Law. With Paloma Capanna, he co-founded Poets for Peace, which sponsors poetry readings across the globe to support relief work. He is the author of a book of poems, *Dancing In Odessa* (2004), which won the Whiting Writer's Award, the American Academy of Arts and Letters' Metcalf Award, and the Dorset Prize. Kaminsky has also received a Ruth Lilly Fellowship, given annually by *Poetry* magazine, and a Lannan Foundation Literary Fellowship. In 2009, poems from his new manuscript, *Deaf Republic*, were awarded *Poetry* magazine's Levinson Prize. He is the co-editor of an anthology of 20th-century poetry in translation, *The Ecco Anthology of International Poetry*. Kaminsky is currently the Director of The Poetry Foundation's Harriet Monroe Poetry Institute.

Mary Karr (b. 1955) was born in Groves, Texas. She is an award-winning poet and best-selling memoirist. She is the author of three best-selling memoirs: *Lit*, *The Liars' Club*, and *Cherry*. Her books of poetry include *Viper Rum* (2001) and *Sinner's Welcome* (2006). A Guggenheim Fellow in poetry, Karr has won Pushcart Prizes for both verse and essays. Other grants include the Whiting Award and Radcliffe's Bunting Fellowship. She is the Peck Professor of Literature at Syracuse University.

Nate Klug (b. 1985) grew up in Wellesley, MA. He is the author of a chapbook of poems, *Consent* (Pressed Wafer, 2012). His poetry and prose have appeared in *The Christian Century*, *Poetry*, *Threepenny Review*, *Yale Review*, and *Zoland Poetry*. Klug attended the University of Chicago and he currently lives in New Haven, CT, where he is a Master of Divinity student at Yale Divinity School and a candidate for ordained ministry in the United Church of Christ.

Li-Young Lee (b. 1957) was born in Jakarta, Indonesia. He emigrated to the U.S. with his family in 1959. He is the recipient of, among numerous awards, three Pushcart Prizes, the Lannan Literary Award, the American Book Award, and the Fellowship of the Academy of American Poets. He has also received the Poetry Society of America's William Carlos Williams Award for *Book of My Nights* (BOA Editions, 2001). Lee has published four books of poetry.

Denise Levertov (1923–1997) was born in Ilford, England. She moved to the U.S. in 1948, and worked as poetry editor for *Mother Jones* magazine and *The Nation*. She published over twenty collections of poetry, four books of prose, and three volumes of poetry translations. Levertov taught at Brandeis University, MIT, the University of Washington, Tufts University, and Stanford University. Among many honors, she received the Shelley Memorial Award, the Robert Frost Medal, the Lenore Marshall Prize, the Lannan Award, a grant from the National Institute of Arts and Letters, a Catherine Luck Memorial grant, and a Guggenheim Fellowship.

Fred Lessing (b. 1936), formerly a professor of philosophy, is a psychologist/therapist in private practice and a hidden child survivor of the Holocaust from The Netherlands. He has four grown children and six grandchildren and lives with his wife Roz in Michigan. He and David Young, his translation collaborator, met in college and became roommates and lifelong friends.

Judy Little (b. 1941) is retired from the English Department at Southern Illinois University and is the author of *Comedy and the Woman Writer* (University of Nebraska Press) and *The Experimental Self* (Southern Illinois Press). Her poetry has appeared in *Beloit Poetry Journal*, *The Anglican Theological Review*, *Vallum*, *Prairie Schooner*, *America*, and *Commonweal*, among other journals.

Marjorie Maddox (b. 1959) is Director of Creative Writing and Professor of English at Lock Haven University. Her books include *Perpendicular As I* (Sandstone Book Award); *Transplant, Transport, Transubstantiation* (Yellowglen Prize); *Weeknights at the Cathedral* (WordTech Editions); *When the Wood Clacks Out Your Name: Baseball*

Poems (Redgreene Press); and six chapbooks. Her poems, stories, and essays have appeared in such journals and anthologies as *Poetry, Prairie Schooner, Crab Orchard Review, American Literary Review, US Catholic, The Art Times, Arabesque: International Literary Journal, Seattle Review, A Fine Frenzy: Poets on Shakespeare,* and *Hurricane Blues: Poems about Katrina and Rita.* She is the co-editor of *Common Wealth: Contemporary Poets on Pennsylvania* (PSU Press, 2005) and the author of two children's books from Boyds Mills Press: *A Crossing of Zebras: Animal Packs in Poetry* (2008) and *Rules of the Game: Baseball Poems* (2009). Her short story collection, *What She Was Saying,* was one of three finalists for the Katherine Anne Porter Book Award. She lives with her husband and two children in Williamsport, PA.

Amit Majmudar (b. 1979) is a diagnostic nuclear radiologist who lives in Columbus, Ohio with his wife and twin sons. His first book, *0°,0° [Zero Degrees, Zero Degrees],* was released by Northwestern University Press/TriQuarterly Books in 2009. His second collection, *Heaven and Earth,* won the 2011 Donald Justice Prize and was published by Story Line Press. His first novel, *Partitions,* was published by Henry Holt/Metropolitan. His poetry has appeared or is forthcoming in *The New Yorker, The Atlantic Monthly, Poetry,* and the 2007 and 2012 *The Best American Poetry* anthologies.

Maurice Manning (b. 1966) teaches at Transylvania University in Lexington, Kentucky and in the M.F.A. Program for Writers at Warren Wilson College. His poems have appeared in *The Southern Review, Virginia Quarterly Review,* and *The New Yorker.* He has published four books of poetry, the most recent of which, *The Common Man,* was one of the two finalists for the 2011 Pulitzer Prize in Poetry. His first book, *Lawrence Booth's Book of Visions,* was chosen by W. S. Merwin for the Yale Series of Younger Poets Award. Manning was a 2011 Guggenheim Fellow.

Ashley Anna McHugh (b. 1985) was born to a working-class military family and raised in a fundamentalist evangelical Christian tradition. Late in her childhood, her father was paralyzed in a hunting accident. Much of her early poetry struggles to reckon with this formative trauma, and with the God who let it come to pass. McHugh's debut collection of poetry, *Into These Knots,* was awarded the 10th annual New Criterion Poetry Prize, and it was released in 2010 by Ivan R. Dee. The title poem of the collection was selected as the winner of the 2009 Morton Marr Poetry Prize. In 2011, LATR Editions released her second book, *Become All Flame,* a limited-edition chapbook. McHugh's poems have appeared in such places as *The New Criterion, Measure, Smartish Pace, The Hopkins Review, Southwest Review, DIAGRAM,* and *Verse Daily.* She is a contributing editor for *Linebreak,* an online journal that she helped to found in 2008. She currently teaches at the University of Arkansas at Fort Smith and resides in Fayetteville, Arkansas.

Philip Memmer (b. 1971) is the author of four books of poems, most recently *The Storehouses of the Snow: Psalms, Parables and Dreams* (Lost Horse Press, 2012). His previous collections include *Lucifer: A Hagiography,* winner of the 2008 Idaho Prize for Poetry from Lost Horse Press, and *Threat of Pleasure* (Word Press, 2008), winner of the 2008 Adirondack Literary Award for Poetry. His poems have appeared in such journals as *Poetry*, *Poetry Northwest*, *Poetry London*, *Southern Poetry Review*, and *Epoch*, as well as in several anthologies. His work has also been featured in the Library of Congress' Poetry 180 project, and in Ted Kooser's *American Life in Poetry* syndicated column. He lives in the rural village of Deansboro, NY, and works as Executive Director of the Arts Branch of the YMCA of Greater Syracuse, where he founded the Downtown Writer's Center in 2001. He also serves as Associate Editor for Tiger Bark Press.

Thomas Merton (1915–1968) was born in Prades, France. Merton converted to Roman Catholicism while at Columbia University, and on December 10, 1941 he entered the Abbey of Gethsemani in Kentucky, a community of monks belonging to the Order of Cistercians of the Strict Observance (Trappists), the most ascetic Roman Catholic monastic order. Merton is the author of more than seventy books, including poetry; social criticism; and writings on peace, justice, and ecumenism. His autobiography, *The Seven Storey Mountain*, has sold over one million copies and has been translated into over fifteen languages. Citing race and peace as the two most urgent issues of our time, Merton was a strong supporter of the nonviolent civil rights movement, which he called "certainly the greatest example of Christian faith in action in the social history of the United States." For his social activism Merton endured severe criticism, from Catholics and non-Catholics alike, who assailed his political writings as unbecoming of a monk. During his last years, he became deeply interested in Asian religions, particularly Zen Buddhism, and in promoting East–West dialogue. After several meetings with Merton during the American monk's trip to Far East in 1968, the Dalai Lama praised him as having a more profound understanding of Buddhism than any other Christian he had known.

Philip Metres (b. 1970) is the author of a number of books, most recently the chapbook *abu ghraib arias* (Flying Guillotine, 2011) and the full-length collection *To See the Earth* (Cleveland State University Poetry Center, 2008). His work has appeared in *Best American Poetry* and has garnered an National Endowment for the Arts Fellowship, a Watson Fellowship, two Ohio Arts Council Grants, and the Cleveland Arts Prize. He teaches literature and creative writing at John Carroll University in Cleveland, Ohio.

Vassar Miller (1924–1998) was born in Houston, Texas. She published her first book of poetry in 1958, which was followed by nine more collections of poetry, as well as an anthology of poetry and stories about persons with disabilities. Vassar suffered from cerebral palsy, which, along with her strong religious convictions, she often explored through poetry. Miller was nominated for a Pulitzer Prize in 1961, named Poet Laureate of Texas in 1982 and 1988, and was named to the Texas Women's Hall of Fame by the Governor's Commission for Women in 1997. She died in Houston in 1998.

Czeslaw Milosz (1911–2004) was born in Szetejnie, Lithuania. He witnessed the Nazi and Stalinist devastation of Lithuania and Poland and he survived World War

II in German-occupied Warsaw with his wife, Janina, publishing his poetry in the underground press. After the war, he was stationed in New York, Washington, and Paris as a cultural attaché from Poland. He defected to France in 1951, and in 1960 he accepted a position at the University of California at Berkeley. He was awarded the Nobel Prize for literature in 1980. He wrote nearly all of his poems in his native Polish, although his work was banned in Poland until after he won the Nobel Prize. He has also translated the works of other Polish writers into English and co-translated his own work with such poets as Robert Hass and Robert Pinsky. His translations into Polish include portions of the Bible (from Hebrew and Greek) and works by Charles Baudelaire, T. S. Eliot, John Milton, William Shakespeare, Simone Weil, and Walt Whitman.

Harry Newman's (b. 1961) poems have been published in *Ecotone, Rattle, Asheville Poetry Review, Fugue, The New Guard*, and many other journals. He was one of the recipients of the 2006 William Stafford Awards as well as a finalist for the 2010 Knightville Poetry Prize. Active in theater, Newman's plays, translations, and performance pieces have been produced at theaters across the country, including the Public Theater/New York Shakespeare Festival, The Kitchen, and the Contemporary American Theater Festival. They have also been presented internationally in The Netherlands and most recently in Germany. He has been playwright-in-residence at the Cincinnati Playhouse in Ohio and a writer-in-residence of the English Department of Utrecht University in Holland. From 2005–2007, he founded and directed The Pool, an interdisciplinary theater workshop, for the Present Company, producers of the New York International Fringe Festival. Newman grew up in Miami and currently lives in Brooklyn.

Hannah Faith Notess (b. 1981) is managing editor of Seattle Pacific University's *Response* magazine and editor of *Jesus Girls: True Tales of Growing Up Female and Evangelical*, a collection of personal essays (Cascade Books, 2009). Her poems have appeared in *The Christian Century, Slate, Crab Orchard Review*, and *Mid-American Review*, among other publications. She lives in Seattle.

Alicia Suskin Ostriker (b. 1937) was born in Brooklyn, New York. She attended Brandeis University and then earned a Ph.D. in literature from the University of Wisconsin–Madison. She is author of twelve volumes of poetry, most recently *The Book of Seventy* (2009), which won the Jewish Book Award for Poetry. Ostriker is the author of numerous volumes of criticism, including *Writing Like a Woman, Stealing the Language: The Emergence of Women's Poetry in America, Feminist Revision and the Bible, The Nakedness of the Fathers: Biblical Visions and Revisions, For the Love of God: The Bible as an Open Book*, and *Dancing at the Devil's Party: Essays on Poetry, Politics and the Erotic*. Ostriker has received awards from the National Endowment for the Arts, the Poetry Society of America, the San Francisco State Poetry Center, the Judah Magnes Museum, the New Jersey Arts Council, the Rockefeller Foundation, and the Guggenheim Foundation. She is Professor Emerita of Rutgers University and is a faculty member of the New England College Low-Residency M.F.A. Program. Ostriker has taught in the Princeton University Creative Writing Program and in Toni Morrison's Atelier Program. She has taught midrash writing workshops in the USA, Israel, England, and Australia. She lives in Princeton, New Jersey with her husband.

Eric Pankey (b. 1959) was born in Kansas City, Missouri. He attended the University of Missouri at Columbia and then earned an M.F.A. from the University of Iowa. When he was 25, his first collection of poems, *For the New Year* (Atheneum), was selected by Mark Strand as the winner of the 1984 Walt Whitman Award. Pankey taught high school English before joining the faculty of Washington University at St. Louis, where he served as Director of the Creative Writing Program. He is the author of *Heartwood* (1988/1998), *Apocrypha* (1991), *The Late Romances* (1997), *Cenotaph* (2000), *Oracle Figures* (2003), *Reliquaries* (2005), and *The Pear As One Example: New and Selected Poems: 1984–2008* (2008). His honors include fellowships from the National Endowment for the Arts, the John Simon Guggenheim Memorial Foundation, and the Ingram Merrill Foundation. He teaches in the Master of Fine Arts Program at George Mason University, where is Professor of English and the Heritage Chair in Writing.

Carl Phillips (b. 1959) is the author of numerous books of poetry: *Double Shadow* (2012), which was awarded the *Los Angeles Times* Book Prize and a National Book Award; *Quiver of Arrows: Selected Poems 1986–2006* (2007); *Riding Westward* (2006); *The Rest of Love* (2004), winner of the Theodore Roethke Memorial Foundation Poetry Prize and the Thom Gunn Award for Gay Male Poetry; *Rock Harbor* (2002); *The Tether* (2001), winner of the Kingsley Tufts Poetry Award; *Pastoral* (2000), winner of the Lambda Literary Award; *From the Devotions* (1998); *Cortège* (1995); and *In the Blood* (1992), winner of the Samuel French Morse Poetry Prize. Phillips is also the author of *Coin of the Realm: Essays on the Art and Life of Poetry* (2004), and the translator of Sophocles's *Philoctetes* (2003). According to the Judges' Citation for the 1998 National Book Awards, for which he was a finalist that year, "Carl Phillips' passionate and lyrical poems read like prayers, with a prayer's hesitations, its desire to be utterly accurate, its occasional flowing outbursts." Phillips is Professor of English and of African and African-American Studies at Washington University in St. Louis, where he also teaches in the Creative Writing Program.

János Pilinszky (1921–1981) was born in Budapest, Hungary, and had a Catholic upbringing and education. He was drafted to serve in the military in 1944; he was captured by the retreating German army and spent the last year of the war in German prison camps in Germany and Austria. What he witnessed in the prison camps had a profound influence on his outlook and his poetry. His first book of poetry, *Trapéz és korlát* [*Trapeze and Bars*], was published in 1946 and was awarded the Baumgarten Prize. It was more than ten years before Pilinszky published another volume of poetry, *Harmadnapon* [*On the Third Day*]. In 1971 he was awarded the Attila Prize for his collection *Nagyvárosi ikonok* [*Metropolitan Icons*], and he published several additional collections before his death in 1981. Two selections of his work have appeared in English: *Selected Poems*, translated by Ted Hughes and János Csokits (Carcanet, 1976)—which was later expanded into *The Desert of Love* (Anvil, 1989)—and *Crater*, translated by Peter Jay (Anvil, 1978). Ted Hughes, in his introduction to *Selected Poems*, notes Pilinszky's complex relationship to religion: "The poems demonstrate [. . .] that his inner relationship to Catholicism is neither simple nor happy. He has been called a Christian poet, even a Catholic poet, and the increasing density of Catholic terminology and imagery in his work provides argument for this. But he rejects those labels absolutely. There is no doubt that he is above all a religious poet. A rather dreadful sun of religious awareness, a midnight sun, hangs over all his responses. But his loyalty to a different order of revelation—which at first seems a directly opposite and contradictory order—comes first."

Stella Vinitchi Radulescu (b. 1946) writes poetry in English, French, and Romanian and is the author of numerous collections of poetry published in the United States, Romania, and France, including *Last Call* (2005), *Diving With the Whales* (2008), *Insomnia in Flowers* (2008), *All Seeds & Blues* (2011), and *I Was Afraid of Vowels . . . Their Paleness* (bilingual, trans. Luke Hankins, 2011). She is the winner of two international poetry prizes awarded by SPAF (Société des Poètes et Artistes de France) for her books published in France, *Terre interrompue* (2007) and *Un cri dans la neige* (2009). Her poems have appeared in *Laurel Review, Asheville Poetry Review, Seneca Review, Pleiades, Rhino, Louisville Review*, and *Spoon River Poetry Review*, among other places, as well as in a variety of literary magazines in France, Belgium, Luxembourg, Québec, and Romania. She holds a Ph.D. in philology from the University of Bucharest and teaches at Northwestern University.

Suzanne Underwood Rhodes (b. 1950) was born in Nyack, New York. Her latest book is a collection of short prose, *A Welcome Shore* (Canon Press, 2010), which was nominated for a Library of Virginia book award. She has published two volumes of poetry with Sow's Ear Press: *What a Light Thing, This Stone* and *Weather of the House*. She is also the author of the poetry textbook, *The Roar on the Other Side* (Canon Press) and a book of prose meditations, *Sketches of Home* (Canon Press). Her poems have appeared in numerous publications, such as *The Alaska Quarterly Review, The Anglican Theological Review, Appalachian Quarterly, Image, Spoon River Poetry Review*, and *Shenandoah*. She works full-time as the director of public affairs for a charitable organization, Mercy Medical Airlift. She has taught writing and literature at various colleges and universities, including Old Dominion University, King College, and East Tennessee State University. She received an M.A. in poetry from Johns Hopkins University and was a resident fellow at the Virginia Center for the Creative Arts. She recently served on the executive committee of the Virginia Poetry Society, is an associate editor for the *Sow's Ear Poetry Review*, and is a co-founder of the Appalachian Center for Poets and Writers. She currently lives in Virginia Beach, Virginia.

Theodore Roethke (1908–1963) was born in Saginaw, Michigan. He attended the University of Michigan and later took some graduate classes at Michigan and Harvard. He was awarded the Pulitzer Prize for his collection of poems, *The Waking*, in 1954. He taught at various colleges and universities, including Lafayette, Pennsylvania State, and Bennington, and lastly at the University of Washington, where he was mentor to a generation of Northwest poets, including David Wagoner, Carolyn Kizer, and Richard Hugo.

Nicholas Samaras (b. 1954) is from a multilingual and multicultural background. He is from Patmos, Greece (the "Island of the Apocalypse"), and at the time of the Greek Junta (the "Coup of the Generals") was brought in exile to be raised further in America. He has lived in Greece, England, Wales, Switzerland, Italy, Germany, Austria, Yugoslavia, Jerusalem, and thirteen states in America; he writes from a place of permanent exile. His first book of poetry, *Hands of the Saddlemaker*, received the Yale Series of Younger Poets Award. His new book of poems, *American Psalm, World Psalm*, is forthcoming from Ashland Poetry Press in 2014. His poems have appeared in *The New Yorker*, *Poetry*, *The Kenyon Review*, and elsewhere. Currently, he lives in West Nyack, New York, where he is completing a memoir of his years living underground.

Michael Schiavo (b. 1976) is the author of *The Mad Song* (Shires Press) and numerous chapbooks, including *Ranges I* (H_NGM_N) and *Ranges II* (Forklift Ink). His poetry has appeared in *CUE*, *The Yale Review*, *The Normal School*, *McSweeney's*, *Fourteen Hills*, *No Tell Motel*, *The Awl*, *Sawmill*, *Drunken Boat*, *jubilat*, *Verse Daily*, and elsewhere. He is the editor of *The Equalizer*, an occasional poetry anthology, and *Gondola*, a print magazine. He lives in Vermont and maintains a blog, The Unruly Servant.

Gjertrud Schnackenberg (b. 1953) was born in Tacoma, Washington. She is the author of six books of poetry: *Portraits and Elegies* (1982), *The Lamplit Answer* (1985), *A Gilded Lapse of Time* (1992), *The Throne of Labdacus* (2000), *Supernatural Love: Poems, 1978–1992* (2000), and *Heavenly Questions* (2011). She is the recipient of the 2000 *Los Angeles Times* Book Prize in Poetry for *The Throne of Labdacus*, the 1998 Academy Award from the American Academy of Arts and Letters, the 2004 Berlin Prize from the American Academy in Berlin, the 1984 Rome Prize in Literature from the American Academy in Rome, and fellowships from the National Endowment for the Arts, The Radcliffe Institute, and the Guggenheim Foundation.

Luci Shaw (b. 1928) was born in London and has lived in Canada, Australia, and the U.S.A. She attended Wheaton College before becoming co-founder and later president of Harold Shaw Publishers. She has been a Writer in Residence at Regent College, Vancouver since 1988. A charter member of the Chrysostom Society of Writers, Shaw is author of ten volumes of poetry, including *Polishing the Petoskey Stone* (1990), *Writing the River* (1994/1997), *The Angles of Light* (2000), *The Green Earth: Poems of Creation* (2002), and *What the Light Was Like* (2006). She has edited three poetry anthologies and a festschrift, *The Swiftly Tilting Worlds of Madeleine L'Engle* (1998). She has also written and co-authored numerous non-fiction books. Shaw is poetry editor and a contributing editor of *Radix*, a quarterly journal published in Berkeley, CA. She is also poetry and fiction editor of *Crux*, an academic journal published quarterly by Regent College. She and her husband live in Bellingham, Washington.

Robert Siegel (b. 1939) graduated from Wheaton College in 1961, and received an M.A. in writing from Johns Hopkins University and a Ph.D. from Harvard University. He has published nine books of poetry and fiction, including the award-winning *Whalesong* trilogy, which has been translated into seven languages. His poetry has received awards from the National Endowment for the Arts, *Poetry, Transatlantic Review*, and the Ingram Merrill Foundation. Siegel has taught at Dartmouth College, Princeton University, Goethe University in Frankfurt, Germany, and for 23 years in the graduate creative writing program at the University of Wisconsin–Milwaukee. He and his wife live near the coast in Maine.

William Stafford (1914–1993) was born in Hutchinson, Kansas. Over the course of his career, Stafford published over 50 books of poetry, prose, and translations, and taught throughout the world. He was the recipient of the National Book Award in 1963 and was named Poet Laureate of the United States in 1970. In 1992, he won the Western States Book Award for lifetime achievement in poetry. In 1975, he was named Poet Laureate of Oregon. He died in 1993 in Lake Oswego, Oregon.

Sofia M. Starnes (b. 1952), a writer of Philippine–Spanish heritage, was born in Manila. She received an advanced degree in English Philology from the University of Madrid and was an English teacher in Spain for 17 years. In 1986, having married an American, she moved to the United States; she became a U.S. citizen in 1989. Starnes is the Poetry Editor of *The Anglican Theological Review* and is the author of four poetry collections: *The Soul's Landscape* (Aldrich Poetry Prize, 2002); *A Commerce of Moments* (Pavement Saw Press, Editor's Prize, 2003; Honor Book in the 2004 Virginia Literary Awards Competition); *Corpus Homini: A Poem for Single Flesh* (Whitebird Poetry Series Prize, Wings Press, 2008), and *Fully Into Ashes* (Wings Press, 2011). She has received various awards for her work, including a Poetry Fellowship from the Virginia Commission for the Arts, the Rainer Maria Rilke Poetry Prize, the *Marlboro Review* Editor's Prize, and a Conference on Christianity and Literature Poetry Prize. In 2009, she was named Distinguished Scholar by Union College, in Barbourville, Kentucky. She currently lives in Williamsburg, Virginia with her husband Bill. : In 2012, Starnes was appointed Poet Laureate of Virginia.

Sufjan Stevens (b. 1975) was born in Detroit and raised in northern Michigan. He attended Hope College and the masters program for writers at the New School for Social Research. He has become well-known in the indie music scene for his unique brand of experimental folk-influenced music and his elaborately staged live shows, including costumes, video projections, animations, dancers, and props. He holds the lofty title of Minster of Aesthetics at Asthmatic Kitty Records. According to the Asthmatic Kitty website, Stevens "mixes autobiography, religious fantasy, and regional history to create folk songs of grand proportions. A preoccupation with epic concepts has motivated two state records (*Michigan* and *Illinois*), an electronic album for the animals of the Chinese zodiac (*Enjoy Your Rabbit*), a five-disc Christmas box set (*Songs for Christmas*), and a programmatic tone poem with film accompaniment for the Brooklyn-Queens Expressway, a large-scale ensemble piece commissioned by BAM in 2007. More recently, Sufjan released two albums in 2010: a generous EP, *All Delighted People*, and the full-length *The Age of Adz*, a collection of songs partly inspired by the outsider artist Royal Robertson."

R. S. Thomas (1913–2000) was born in Cardiff and spent his boyhood in the port town of Holyhead on the Isle of Anglesey, but most of his life was spent in remote rural and coastal areas of north Wales, where he worked as an Anglican priest and wrote some of the most important religious poetry of the 20th century. Thomas came to believe in what he called "the true Wales of my imagination," a Welsh-speaking, aboriginal, Celtic community living in harmony with nature. Feeling alienated from this culture, he learned the Welsh language and wrote his autobiography in Welsh. He could tolerate neither the English who bought up Wales and, in his view, stripped it of its wild, essential nature, nor the servile Welsh who kowtowed to English money and influence. In the 1960s, his very public socio-political positions made him an increasingly controversial figure and a cultural icon. Despite his public voice, Thomas's greatest poetry is a personal wrestling with spiritual immensities. Spiritual concerns were always part of his poetry, but his later poetry in particular (written during the 1970s and beyond) is a sustained religious questioning, a searching for an absent God, a struggle to accept God's refusal to commune with mankind, and an experiment with metaphoric representations of God. More than any British poet of his generation, he experimented with the metaphoric possibilities of science and technology in relation to questions of faith. For his uncompromising devotion to his ideals, R. S. Thomas was nominated for the Nobel Prize in 1996.

M. Vasalis (1909–1998) was a Dutch poet and psychiatrist. M. Vasalis is the pseudonym of Margaretha Droogleever Fortuyn-Leenmans. Vasalis is her Latinized maiden name. Vasalis studied medicine and anthropology at Leiden University and in 1939 established herself as psychiatrist in Amsterdam and later in Assen. Vasalis made her debut in 1940 with the collection *Parken en woestijnen* [*Parks and Deserts*]. Her other poetry collections are *De vogel Phoenix* [*The Bird Phoenix*] (1947) and *Vergezichten en gezichten* [*Views and Faces*] (1954).

Robert Penn Warren (1905–1989) was born in Guthrie, Kentucky. At Vanderbilt University in 1921 he became the youngest member of the group of Southern poets called the Fugitives, which included John Crowe Ransom, Allen Tate, Donald Davidson, and Merrill Moore—a group that advocated the rural Southern agrarian tradition and classical aesthetic ideals in poetry and criticism. Warren later taught at Vanderbilt University, Louisiana State University, The University of Minnesota, and Yale University. With Cleanth Brooks, he co-authored *Understanding Poetry* (1938), a textbook that widely influenced the study of poetry in many America universities. Warren was also a novelist and won the Pulitzer Prize for his novel *All the King's Men* in 1947. Over time, Warren's poetry became less formal and more expansive, and he began to earn many accolades: his *Promises: Poems, 1954–1956* won the Sidney Hillman Award, the Edna St. Vincent Millay Memorial Award, the National Book Award, and the Pulitzer Prize. In 1979 he earned a third Pulitzer Prize for *Now and Then: Poems, 1976–1978*. Warren served as a Chancellor of The Academy of

American Poets from 1972 until 1988, and was selected as a MacArthur Fellow in 1981. Warren was named the first U.S. Poet Laureate Consultant in Poetry in 1986.

Daniel Westover (b. 1975) grew up in the American West (Utah, Idaho, Oregon, California) before eventually settling in East Tennessee. In the mid-1990s, he spent two years as a missionary in Bulgaria, working in orphanages, teaching English classes, and volunteering in religious congregations. He later earned an M.F.A. in poetry from McNeese State University before going abroad once more, this time to the Isle of Anglesey in Wales, where he lived while completing a Ph.D. at the University of Wales. He is author of *R. S. Thomas: A Stylistic Biography* (University of Wales Press, 2011) and co-editor of a recent issue of *Literature and Belief*, dedicated to the work of Welsh poet Leslie Norris. His biography of Norris is in preparation and under contract with Parthian Books. Daniel is also author of *Toward Omega* (21st Editions, 2005), a book of poems featuring photographs by Vincent Serbin. His poems have appeared in *North American Review, Southeast Review, Asheville Poetry Review, Measure, Crab Orchard Review, Spoon River Poetry Review, Tar River Poetry,* and *The Southern Poetry Anthology*. He lives with his wife Mary and their two daughters, Eden and Branwen, in Johnson City, Tennessee, where he is Assistant Professor of Modern British literature at East Tennessee State University.

Richard Wilbur (b. 1921) was raised in North Caldwell, New Jersey. He graduated from Amherst College in 1942, and attended graduate school at Harvard University. He has published seventeen collections of poetry, five children's books, and various works of prose and translations. Wilbur has been the recipient of numerous honors over the course of his 60-year career, including an appointment as U.S. Poet Laureate in 1987, two Pulitzer Prizes for poetry, the National Book Award, the Edna St. Vincent Millay Award, the Bollingen Prize, and the Chevalier, Ordre National des Palmes Académiques. In 1994 he received the National Medal of Arts from President Clinton. Wilbur currently lives in Cummington, Massachusetts, and Key West, Florida.

Christian Wiman (b. 1966) is the author of three collections of poems, *The Long Home* (1998; reissued in 2007), *Hard Night* (2005), and *Every Riven Thing* (2010), as well as a collection of essays, *Ambition and Survival: Becoming a Poet* (2007). He is the translator and editor of *Stolen Air: Selected Poems of Osip Mandelstam* (2012). Wiman has served as Editor of *Poetry* magazine since 2003. He suffers from a rare and life-threatening form of cancer, which has caused him much pain and many hospital stays. He lives in Chicago with his wife.

Charles Wright (b. 1935) was born in Pickwick Dam, Tennessee. He was educated at Davidson College and the University of Iowa Writers' Workshop. He began to read and write poetry while stationed in Italy during his four years of service in the U.S. Army, and published his first collection of poems, *The Grave of the Right Hand*, in 1970. His second and third collections, *Hard Freight* (1973) and *Country Music: Selected Early Poems* (1983), were both nominated for National Book Awards; the latter received the prize. Since then, Wright has published numerous collections of poems, including *Outtakes* (2010); *Sestets: Poems* (2009); *Littlefoot: A Poem* (2008); *Scar Tissue* (2007), which was the international winner for the Griffin Poetry Prize; *Buffalo Yoga* (2004); *Appalachia* (1998); *Black Zodiac* (1997), which won the Pulitzer Prize and the *Los Angeles Times* Book Prize; *Chickamauga* (1995), which won the Lenore Marshall Poetry Prize from the Academy of American Poets; *The World of the Ten Thousand Things: Poems 1980–1990* (1990); and *Zone Journals* (1988). Wright has also written two volumes of criticism: *Halflife* (1988) and *Quarter Notes* (1995), and has translated the work of Dino Campana in *Orphic Songs* (1984) as well as Eugenio Montale's *The Storm and Other Poems* (1978), which was awarded the PEN Translation Prize. His many honors include the American Academy of Arts and Letters Award of Merit Medal and the Ruth Lilly Poetry Prize. In 1999 he was elected a Chancellor of The Academy of American Poets. He is Souder Family Professor of English at the University of Virginia in Charlottesville.

Franz Wright (b. 1953) is the author of numerous collections of poetry, including *The Beforelife* (2001); *Walking to Martha's Vineyard*, which won the Pulitzer Prize in 2004; *God's Silence* (2006); and *Kindertotenwald* (2011), a collection of prose poems. He has received a Whiting Fellowship and grants from the National Endowment for the Arts. Wright has translated poetry by Rainer Maria Rilke and René Char; in 2008 he and his wife, Elizabeth Oehlkers Wright, co-translated a collection by the Belarusian poet Valzhyna Mort, *Factory of Tears*. Franz Wright's father was the Pulitzer Prize-winning poet James Wright. He has taught at Emerson College and other universities, has worked in mental health clinics, and has volunteered at a center for grieving children.

C. Dale Young (b. 1969) practices medicine full-time, serves as Poetry Editor of the *New England Review*, and teaches in the Warren Wilson College M.F.A. Program for Writers. He is the author of *The Day Underneath the Day* (TriQuarterlyBooks, 2001), *The Second Person* (Four Way Books, 2007), and *Torn* (Four Way Books, 2011). He has been awarded a Guggenheim fellowship, the Grolier Prize, the Tennessee Williams Scholarship in Poetry from the Sewanee Writers' Conference, both the Stanley P. Young Fellowship and Amanda Davis Fellowship from the Bread Loaf Writers' Conference, and a creative writing fellowship from the National Endowment for the Arts. He lives in San Francisco with his spouse, the biologist and composer Jacob Bertrand.

David Young (b. 1936) is author of many books of poetry and prose, including *Field of Light and Shadow*, *Imagining Shakespeare's Pericles*, and *Seasoning: A Poet's Year*, and is an editor of the literary magazine *FIELD* and at Oberlin College Press. He delights in translating (Rilke, Celan, Petrarch, Montale, Du Fu, etc.) and in the kind of collaboration he has had with Fred Lessing, his college roommate of many years ago.

Permissions

Malaika King Albrecht: "On the Shore of Holden Beach" and "Sound Knows its Place in the Air" are reprinted from *What the Trapeze Artist Trusts* (Press 53), copyright © 2012 by Malaika King Albrecht, by permission of the author.

Agha Shahid Ali: "God" and "Film *Bhajan* Found on a 78 RPM" are reprinted from *Rooms Are Never Finished*, copyright © 2002 by Agha Shahid Ali, by permission of W. W. Norton & Company, Inc.

Yehuda Amichai: "Near the Wall of a House" and "Relativity" are reprinted from *The Selected Poetry of Yehuda Amichai*, edited and translated by Chana Bloch and Stephen Mitchell, copyright © 1996 by Chana Bloch and Stephen Mitchell, by permission of the University of California Press.

A. R. Ammons: "Hymn" is reprinted from *Collected Poems: 1951–1971*, copyright © 1960 by A. R. Ammons, by permission of W. W. Norton & Company, Inc.

W. H. Auden: The excerpt from "The More Loving One," copyright © 1957 by W. H. Auden and renewed 1985 by The Estate of W. H. Auden, from *Collected Poems of W. H. Auden*, is reprinted in North America by permission of Random House, Inc. It is reprinted from *Homage to Clio*, copyright © 1960 by W. H. Auden, renewed by The Estate of W. H. Auden, in the United Kingdom/British Commonwealth by permission of Curtis Brown, Ltd.

Bruce Beasley: "Damaged Self-Portrait" is reprinted from *Signs and Abominations*, copyright © 2000 by Bruce Beasley, by permission of Wesleyan University Press (www.wesleyan.edu/wespress).

Wendell Berry: "To Know the Dark" and "The Hidden Singer" are reprinted from *The Selected Poems of Wendell Berry*, copyright © 1998 by Wendell Berry, by permission of Counterpoint Press.

John Berryman: "9" from "Eleven Addresses to the Lord" is reprinted from *Collected Poems: 1937–1971*, copyright © 1989 by Kate Donahue Berryman, in North America by permission of Farrar, Straus and Giroux, LLC, and in the United Kingdom/British Commonwealth by permission of Faber and Faber Ltd.

Justin Bigos and Luke Hankins: "An Interview with Luke Hankins" originally appeared on the *American Literary Review* blog and is reprinted by permission of Justin Bigos and Luke Hankins.

Malachi Black: "Sext," "Vespers," and "Matins" are reprinted from *Quarantine* (Argos Books), copyright © 2012 by Malachi Black, by permission of the author.

Permissions

Permissions

About the Editor

LUKE HANKINS (B. 1984) is the author of a book of poems, *Weak Devotions* (Wipf & Stock, 2011). His chapbook of translations of French poems by Stella Vinitchi Radulescu, *I Was Afraid of Vowels . . . Their Paleness*, was published in 2011 by Q Avenue Press. He is Senior Editor at *Asheville Poetry Review*, where he has served on staff since 2006. He earned an M.F.A. at Indiana University, where he held The Yusef Komunyakaa Fellowship in Poetry. His poems, essays, and translations have appeared in numerous publications, including *American Literary Review*, *Contemporary Poetry Review*, *New England Review*, *Poetry East*, *Verse Daily*, and *The Writer's Chronicle*, as well as on the American Public Media radio program *On Being*.